TERESA OF CALCUTTA
Serving the Poorest of the Poor

by D. Jeanene Watson

Agnes and her family lived in Macedonia in eastern Europe. Agnes eagerly read letters by missionaries from faraway places. She especially enjoyed the letters from Calcutta, India.

Eventually Agnes arrived in Calcutta where she taught young, well-to-do girls. They knew her as Sister Teresa. Unsatisfied, Teresa searched for her calling in life. One day she decided to work with "the poorest of the poor." She conducted her first class in a public park. Only five street children attended. Despite the hardships, she stayed with the work. She knew that God had sent her to care for these people who had no one else to love them.

Teresa dressed in a simple white sari with a blue border. A safety pin held a cross at her left shoulder. She became a familiar sight in the slum streets of Calcutta.

Teresa not only helped the poor, she became one of them. She told the girls she trained, "We will pattern our lives after their poverty. We are poor by choice. We want to be poor like Christ, who, being rich, chose to be born and live and work among the poor."

ABOUT THE AUTHOR

D. Jeanene Watson is a Christian who gave her heart to Jesus at an early age. She is active in church work. For more than ten years she has served as a sponsor of a church organization that trains girls in every aspect of Christian service, with special emphasis upon the work of missionaries. For four years, Jeanene served as coordinator of the program.

D. Jeanene Watson has a graduate degree in communications from Webster College in St. Louis. Her undergraduate degree is a B.A. from Harris State College, Missouri. At present she teaches remedial reading to elementary children. She has also taught mathematics on the high school level.

Jeanene makes her home in High Ridge, Missouri, with her husband and two children.

ABOUT THE ARTIST

Robert E. Lawson lives in Kalamazoo, Michigan, where he draws covers for books and enjoys working on all kinds of art.

Rob was pleased to do the artwork for this book, as he has always admired Mother Teresa and the work she does.

Teresa of Calcutta

Serving the Poorest of the Poor

by

D. Jeanene Watson

Illustrated by **Robert Lawson**

MOTT MEDIA

Milford, Michigan 48042

COPYRIGHT © 1984 by Mott Media

Louise H. Rock, Editor
A. G. Smith, Cover Artist

LIBRARY OF CONGRESS CATALOGING IN PUBLICATION DATA

Watson, D. Jeanene
    Teresa of Calcutta: Serving the Poorest of the Poor.

    (The Sowers)
    Bibliography: p. 167
    Includes Index.

    SUMMARY: A biography of the founder of the Missionary Sisters and Brothers of Charity, known for her work with the destitute and dying in the streets and slums of Calcutta and other cities.
    1. Teresa, Mother, 1910- —Juvenile literature. 2. Nuns—India—Calcutta—Biography—Juvenile literature. 3. Calcutta (India)—Biography—Juvenile literature. 4. Missionaries of Charity—Juvenile literature. [1. Teresa, Mother, 1910- 2. Nuns. 3. Missionaries. 4. Missions—India] I. Lawson, Robert (Rob), ill. II. Title.

BX4406.5.Z8W36 1984   271'.97 [B] [92]   84-60313
ISBN 0-88062-013-7 Hardbound
ISBN 0-88062-012-9 Paperbound

DEDICATION

To my husband, without whose help
this book would not have been possible.

Acknowledgments

Special thanks must be given to two people who made this book possible. First, the Sower books exist only because Mr. George Mott conceived of the series and saw the first books through to publication. Second, Father William B. Faherty, the author of several award winning books, encouraged me to write the biography of Teresa of Calcutta.

I would also like to thank Brian Forney of the reference department of Pope Pius XII Library for his help. Many others have provided valuable information, and their aid is greatly appreciated, too.

CONTENTS

Preface

Few people have won the admiration of the world as fully as Teresa of Calcutta. Her story is full of twists and turns, unexpected good fortune, and heart-rending decisions. But most of all, her life is alive with the joy of Christian service.

Teresa began the Missionaries of Charity to serve "Christ in disguise," her term for the poor. My goal in writing this book is to capture the spirit and excitement of her work.

Touch *your* life with someone special. Read about Teresa of Calcutta.

—*D. Jeanene Watson*

LET ME SOW LOVE . . .

Lord, make me an instrument of Your peace,
Where there is hatred, let me sow love;
Where there is injury, pardon;
Where there is doubt, faith;
Where there is despair, hope;
Where there is darkness, light;
And where there is sadness, joy.

O divine Master, grant that I may not
So much seek to be consoled as to console;
To be understood as to understand;
To be loved as to love;
For it is in giving that we receive;
It is in pardoning that we are pardoned;
And it is in dying
That we are born to eternal life.

AMEN
—St. Francis of Assisi

CALCUTTA

Where Cross and Crescent Meet

At first, Agnes Bojaxhiu did not notice her brother's strange conduct. Lazar Bojaxhiu normally walked home with everyone else after classes at Gimnaziya, the government school. But this afternoon he trailed along behind the group, his face furrowed in deep and troubled thought.

As the long winter of 1919 ended in Skopje, Macedonia, the weather grew more delightful every day. Agnes looked up at the clouds. Patches of blue showed through, and on the western horizon the sky cleared entirely.

Agnes asked Aga, her sister, "Can we have a picnic tomorrow?"

The other students listened for Aga's answer, too. She was the oldest and the smartest. Even Lazar let her plan their afterschool activities.

Aga Bojaxhiu took her task of leadership seriously. She examined the clouds and noticed the clear blue

in the west. "The weather will be good tomorrow,"
she decided. "Let's meet at the bridge after classes.
Everybody bring something to eat."

"I'll bring my accordion," Agnes said. "We'll sing
songs and have a great time."

Enrico Antoni, a friend of the Bojaxhiu family,
agreed right away. He played the violin and loved to
sing. "What about Lazar?" Enrico asked.

Agnes looked back and wondered what could be the
matter with her brother. She slowed her steps and fell
behind to join Lazar. She asked, "Doesn't a picnic
sound good?"

Lazar, however, only grunted. After a moment he
spoke. He sounded as if he were talking more to
himself than to his sister. "Father is in danger."

Agnes drew in her breath. "Why do you say such
a terrible thing?" she asked. "Father is a successful
businessman, and all of the Albanians in Skopje come
to him when they need help. Hundreds of people count
him as their best friend."

"There are just as many people who consider him
their enemy," Lazar said. He reached down and
picked up a chip of stone from the cobblestone street.
He threw the pebble far out over the Vardar River
and watched as it plunked into the cold water. Finally
he said, "He's a target now for those who disagree
with his political views."

"Why do you say he is in danger?" Agnes
demanded. "What proof do you have?"

Lazar pulled his thick, homespun vest closer and
shrugged. He held out his hands helplessly. "There
is no proof. I just feel it!"

"I won't listen to you!" said Agnes. "You're trying to spoil our picnic!"

She skipped ahead and joined the others.

By the time they reached the ancient stone bridge

across the Vardar River she'd put the matter out of her mind. Even Lazar brightened and walked with the rest of the group.

The buildings and homes of Skopje stood on both sides of the Vardar River, with only the bridge to connect them. In one direction, a farmer's team of mules pulled a wagon filled with bales of straw. From the other direction, a trader led a string of hardy little donkeys, each loaded with a backpack. A woman carrying a staff kept a yoke of tired, sleepy-eyed oxen moving. Occasionally, a gasoline powered auto would rattle across the uneven roadbed.

The students said goodbye and ran home. Some disappeared into the old quarter, the older part of the city, where second-story balconies of the Turkish houses overlooked narrow, crooked lanes. Other students crossed the bridge to the city square. They lived in the modern part of Skopje.

Agnes and her brother and sister strolled through the marketplace. Street venders called out their wares: copper pots and pans, silver bells and candlesticks, straw baskets and clay pots.

Shopkeepers welcomed the warm weather. They stepped outside their unlighted booths to talk with one another and with their customers. One woman set up her spinning wheel in the open air and spun while keeping an eye on the store.

Food was for sale, too—sweets, minced meats, roasted hot peppers, smoked fish, herbs and spices. Pushcarts with charcoal fires sent up the fragrance of cooking food.

People from many nations squeezed between the crowded stalls—Albanians in white skull caps, peasants in rough homespun, gypsy women in baggy pantaloons, Turks wearing bright red fez caps, and Italians dressed in business suits.

The people spoke a half dozen different languages as they bargained about the prices. Added to this was the bleat of sheep, the clang of bells on goats, dogs barking, the tap-tap-tap of a shoe cobbler, and the sizzle of food being cooked.

"Everything is so alive!" exclaimed Agnes, overwhelmed by the sounds and smells.

Aga cautioned, "Hurry up. We'll be late for the Sodality meeting."

Reluctantly, Agnes followed her sister.

The Bojaxhiu family lived in one of the two houses that Nikola Bojaxhiu owned. The second house he rented to others.

Nikola and an Italian friend ran a construction firm in Skopje, and it was quite successful. The money from the rented house, added to the business income, meant that the Bojaxhiu family lacked for nothing.

The garden separated the two Bojaxhiu houses. The building they lived in had two floors, with walls of plastered brick painted blue on the outside, and white trim around the windows. Wooden shingles covered the steeply sloping roof. A white cross stood between the tiny upstairs windows.

If Nikola Bojaxhiu could be described as a man of business and politics, his wife Dronda could be described as a woman of religion.

Dronda told her children, "Since Skopje has no Catholic school you must attend the government school. But after school you will attend classes at the parish church."

As it turned out, Agnes and Aga enjoyed the church classes so much they joined Sodality, the religious society for girls.

Their mother could not have been more pleased.

"We enjoy Sodality," Aga said. "The choir, the classes, the worship services—"

"And the letters from missionaries," Agnes said. "I like them most of all."

This afternoon Agnes and Aga stopped at home only long enough to leave their school books. They left right away for the Sodality meeting.

They attended the meetings at the Albanians' Catholic church of Skopje. It was not the city's best-known church. That honor belonged to the Church of the Holy Savior with its magnificent wooden bell tower. Inside, detailed scenes from the Bible were carved in wooden panels. The Church of the Holy Savior stood on ground that had been dug below street level.

"Why are so many of the Catholic churches dug into the ground?" Agnes asked at the Sodality meeting.

The parish priest explained, "Until a few years ago the Turks ruled Macedonia. They follow the Moslem religion. They refused to let any place of worship other than a mosque rise above the other buildings. At one time Skopje had more than three hundred Moslem mosques. Many of the mosques are still in use, although some have fallen into ruin."

The better mosques had intricate geometric patterns on their rounded domes, lattice-work windows, expensive carpets on their floors, and tall spire towers with clocks that kept Mecca time.

The parish priest continued, "Skopje is known as the city where Cross and Crescent meet. The symbol of the Christian religion is the cross. The Moslems have a symbol, too, the crescent moon. Skopje has many faiths, quite unlike any other city in Europe. Catholics, Greek Orthodox, and Moslem religions all find expression in our city."

As the meeting came to a close, the priest said, "I've saved the best for last—a letter from Brother Anthony in India."

Going to the wall he pulled down a giant map of the world. He pointed to Skopje and Macedonia. "Macedonia was a mission area long ago. At the mouth of the Vardar River is Thessalonike. The books of First and Second Thessalonians in the New Testament are actually letters that Paul wrote to the Christians in Thessalonike. The physician Luke, author of the Gospel of Luke and of the Book of Acts, is believed to have been a citizen of Macedonia. Paul and Luke wrote about their travels. So do missionaries of today."

He held up the letter. "Brother Anthony writes about the Bengal mission in India." The priest pointed to India on the map. "He lives in Darjeeling, near the Himalaya mountains."

As the priest read the letter, Agnes listened, fascinated by Brother Anthony's mission work in India. New churches were being built in Calcutta; a Bible school was started in Kurseong; clinics and homes for orphans were established in the Ganges Delta. Agnes rested her chin on her hands and closed her eyes. Those faraway places had such mysterious names!

After the meeting Agnes walked to the map and pointed out all of the places from which other missionaries had written: the Philippines, South America, Africa, and India.

"I've never met a missionary," Agnes admitted, "but I remember all their letters. I remember everything they do and every place they go."

The priest said, "Brother Anthony is from Yugoslavia. When he visits home, I'll invite him to come and tell about his work in person."

As Agnes left the church, Tanja Ruzicka, who had
only recently joined Sodality, spoke, "Agnes?"

"Yes?" Agnes stopped to see what Tanja wanted.
The girl carried her head half bowed and seldom
looked anyone in the eyes. She said, "My grades at
school . . . I am afraid I'll fail geography."

Agnes didn't answer.

The girl plunged ahead. "Will you help me with
my homework?"

"Why do you ask for my help?" asked Agnes. "My
sister is the smart one in our family."

"Please," begged Tanja. "You make good grades
in geography. You could help—if you wanted to."

Agnes shrugged. "Perhaps I don't care to help,"
she said. "Doing my own schoolwork is boring enough
without helping someone else do theirs as well."

"But . . . ." Tanja's voice trailed to a stop. Tears
brimmed in her eyes.

For a moment Agnes understood the problem the
girl faced. Tanja Ruzicka didn't have the comfort of
a well-to-do home. The daughters of poor people were
expected to labor in the fields, till the soil, watch flocks
and herds. Tanja would not be at the picnic tomorrow. She'd have to stay home and work. For this girl,
a good education meant escape from the world of
poverty. She had to do well in school.

"Next week," Agnes said. "Maybe I'll have time
to help you next week—unless you can find someone
else before then."

The girl brightened. "Oh, thanks!" And Tanja
skipped away happy.

Why did I promise to help, Agnes wondered. Still,
in a week much could happen. Maybe Tanja would
find someone else.

When Agnes arrived home, Aga was in the kitchen
making a list of food to take on the picnic.

Later the family gathered at the table for the evening meal. Dronda prepared a table full of food. The meal began with chicken soup and fresh bread. Then Dronda served a green salad with vinegar and oil dressing. For the main course they ate meat and rice rolled in cabbage and boiled potatoes fried in oil, with milk to drink.

During the meal, Lazar announced his decision to join the army when he became old enough. "A soldier is one person who can expect employment in Macedonia," he said. "From the beginning, Macedonia has been fought over, first by Illyrians, then Huns, Romans, Byzantines, Slavs, and Turks. The fighting is not likely to stop now."

Agnes suspected her brother was right. When she was born in 1910, Skopje was part of the Turkish Ottoman Empire. In 1912, the first Balkan War broke out in Macedonia and a year later Skopje was liberated from the Turks and became a part of Serbia.

Within a few months, however, another and larger war swept across Europe, and Skopje changed hands again. This Great War of the Nations (World War I) ended with Skopje becoming a part of Yugoslavia. For ten years the people of the area had suffered through an almost constant state of war.

As Lazar talked, he continued eating. Soon he was ready for dessert.

Dronda served Nikola strong, black coffee in a small cup. For Lazar she had fresh apple juice. And for both of them a piece of cake frosted with pudding.

Agnes and Aga helped clear the table.

A knock sounded at the door. A stranger entered and asked to speak with Nikola. Nikola joined him in the front room.

Later that night, as Agnes prepared for bed she

heard the sound of the stranger and her father still talking downstairs.

"The house is always full of visitors," Agnes complained. "They talk constantly of Albania and its independence."

Her father often said, "We suffered terribly at the hands of the Turks. Now, I intend to look out for our affairs." He held meetings in the Bojaxhiu home that lasted well into the night. Men who did not give their names came after dark and when the secret talks ended, they disappeared into the night.

Now Aga explained, "Father grew up in Albania and only moved to Yugoslavia after he and Mother married. Albania is his country, and its future is important to him."

Agnes climbed into bed and pulled the covers up to her chin. She said, "Yugoslavia, and not Albania, is my home. I don't understand what the fuss is about."

The next day proved Aga to be a good weather forecaster. The sun shone in a cloudless sky. Sunlight splashed down warm and bright on the town of Skopje.

After school the students met at the Vardar bridge.

"Where shall we go for the picnic?" Enrico asked.

Aga said, "Remember where the old Ottoman aqueduct passes near the ruins of the Roman fortress?"

"Yes," Enrico said. "I know the place. A stream is nearby and a line of trees is along the edge of the field. It will be the perfect spot for a picnic!"

The others nodded.

The rolling fields outside Skopje became more and more rugged until they grew into the lofty heights of the distant mountains. The fields would soon be planted in wheat and other crops. For now only an occasional tree or the lines of ancient fence rows marked them.

Along the way the group passed a crude one-room building, the home of a peasant family. Twisted poles made the walls. Dried mud and stones filled in the gaps. A straw roof completed the primitive hut. A pair of storks stood on the roof.

Agnes wondered aloud, "Could the people living there be Catholic, Moslem, or Greek Orthodox? There's no way to know by looking at their house."

Aga said, "The poor look alike and live in the same desperate condition regardless of their religion."

When the group arrived at the agreed upon spot, Sophia and Yelena cleared a level space. Aga and Agnes began laying out the tablecloth and spreading the food—ham, cheese, crusty bread, and apples, with mineral water to drink and cookies for dessert.

Lazar, Enrico, Ivan, and Sasha promptly marked out a race course and challenged each other to foot races. When they grew tired of that they found a huge stone the size of a small boulder and took turns try ing to throw it the farthest.

Eventually the contests made the boys hungry. Enrico came back and asked, "Can we eat now?"

Aga said, "Everyone sit down around the tablecloth. We'll all eat together."

When they finished, Enrico noticed the sun as it cast the long shadows of late afternoon. "Let me take a photograph before the light gets too dim," he said.

Agnes and the other girls sat on the ground. Aga held her parasol and stood beside them.

Lazar, Ivan, and Sasha looked on in a studied lack of interest.

Enrico took great pains to compose the picture just right. He ordered them to move this way and that. He prized his camera and prided himself upon how many of the pictures he took turned out well.

As Agnes smiled at the camera, she saw Lazar standing behind Enrico. Her brother's face, puckered in thought, held the same expression as yesterday when he worried about their father.

Agnes held the frozen smile as Enrico clicked the camera.

But as the sunlight faded and the air grew chilly, she shivered at the thought of what would happen to their happy family if something terrible befell her father.

CALCUTTA

Follow Your Own Road

Agnes woke up in the middle of the night at the sound of her mother's footsteps walking quickly to the front door. The door creaked and her mother's frightened voice sounded sharp and loud in the silent house.

"Oh, doctor!" her mother said. "He's sick, very sick. Come! This way."

The doctor's voice rumbled soothing words.

In the darkness Agnes whispered to her sister, "What's the matter?"

Aga didn't answer.

Agnes looked over and saw Aga's covers thrown back. The bed was empty. Her sister's slippers and robe were missing.

Agnes jumped out of bed, tossed a robe around her shoulders, and ran to the steps.

A yellow glow from the lamps lighted the landing at the bottom of the stairs. As she started down, Aga motioned her back.

"Why?" Agnes asked. "Who needs a doctor?" She walked on down the stairs.

"Father," Aga explained. "He is sick. Something he ate disagreed with him. The doctor thinks it is food poisoning."

Agnes reached the end of the steps. She saw the doctor and her mother beside her father, who lay on the couch. A thin film of perspiration made his forehead glossy. His eyes darted from side to side. His breath came in gasps.

Nikola's lips moved, but only a croaking sound came out. His fingers twitched.

Dronda assured him. "The doctor is here. Lie back. Do what he says."

Dronda told the girls, "Go back upstairs and to bed. There is nothing you can do."

Reluctantly, Agnes retraced her steps. "What happened?" she asked.

Aga explained, "Father attended a banquet tonight. The food must have been tainted. He came home and barely staggered into the front room before falling to his knees. Mother sent Lazar for the doctor right away."

"Will he be all right?" Agnes asked.

Aga didn't answer at first. Finally she said, "I've never seen anyone look as sick as he does."

Agnes lay in her bed and listened to the activity on the floor below. The front door opened and closed several times. Neighbors arrived. The number of voices grew.

Once she heard the doctor direct some men to move Nikola. Then the house grew silent. Either the people downstairs had stopped talking, or they were speaking in whispers.

The next morning Agnes awoke confused. She remembered the events of the night before as if it were a dream.

Then she looked over at Aga. Her sister sat on the side of the bed, her body shaking with great silent sobs. "He died. Father died during the night."

The next five days passed as a dull ache for Agnes. Afterward, she could recall only disconnected scenes— women dressed all in black, the heavy scent of flowers, a wooden coffin, slow mournful songs, and her mother's red-rimmed eyes.

And Lazar. "Father was murdered!" her brother said bitterly.

The doctor disagreed. "Your father died of a clear case of food poisoning. Nothing else."

"Yes, poisoning. But not an accident," Lazar persisted.

The doctor only shook his head. "All of the evidence points to a tragic case of food that contained a deadly germ."

"A political enemy killed father," Lazar slammed his fist into the palm of his hand. "For as long as I live I'll never believe otherwise."

No one else took her brother's suspicions seriously. Agnes herself accepted the doctor's report.

But her father had eaten the food at a political rally. Too often political quarrels led nowhere except to trouble. "I won't have anything to do with politics," she decided.

Agnes wondered if the pain of her father's death would ever be erased. Food lost its taste. The songs she loved to sing sounded out of tune. Every day seemed somehow overcast.

She returned to school and sat through her classes. She listened to the lectures without really hearing. She looked at the blackboard without really seeing. Finally, the day ended and she started home.

"Agnes." A voice broke into her dark thoughts.

"Eh?" Agnes asked.

"It's me, Tanja Ruzicka," the girl said. "I'm sorry to hear about your father."

Agnes merely nodded.

The girl waited, expectantly.

Then Agnes remembered her promise to help Tanja with homework. "You still want me to help you with the geography? After what has happened?"

"Please forgive me for bothering you," Tanja lowered her eyes and looked at her feet. "I really do need your help. Say you will."

Agnes didn't have the spirit to argue or make excuses. "Very well. But I warn you that I won't be much help."

They sat under a tree on the school ground. Opening the geography book, Agnes turned to the maps and pointed out the capital cities, lakes, mountain ranges, and river valleys. She described something interesting about each and made up questions about the surrounding countries: Greece, Bulgaria, Romania, Austria, and Hungary. She corrected Tanja's mistakes and encouraged her when she gave the right answers.

Eventually Tanja said, "Thank you for helping. I must go home now."

Agnes checked the time. In amazement she realized they had worked together for more than an hour. During that time the dull ache of her father's death left. She actually found herself humming a favorite tune—and enjoying it.

But her father's death did leave the family in a desperate condition.

Aga couldn't understand. "Everyone pointed to father as a successful businessman. His construction firm earned a good profit."

Their mother explained the true situation, "Your father gave money to this cause or that. He put very little aside in savings."

"What will we do?" Agnes asked.

In reply, Dronda began singing a simple song:

> Put your hand in His, In His hand,
> And walk all the way along with Him.

Dronda assured them, "We'll trust in Jesus. He will provide."

Agnes wanted to believe her mother, but Dronda appeared to be showing more courage than she actually felt.

Dronda continued talking, making plans for the future. "I'll organize an embroidery and handicraft business. But I'm afraid we'll have to sell the house."

Aga drew back in dismay. "Sell our house!"

Dronda soothed her. "Not this one, but the one we rent. We'll use the money so you two can stay in

school until you graduate. I know that most girls do
not finish secondary school. But my daughters will
be exceptions. A good education will prepare you for
the future."

Agnes became more earnest in her school work and
in church activities. Before, when her father lived,
Agnes seldom excelled at school. She enjoyed playing too much. She had a reputation as a fun loving
tomboy—and rather spoiled.

Afterward, she never lost her sense of humor. But
she showed a serious side now. She began helping
other students whenever she could. Her grades
improved.

Soon Agnes would enter high school, and she would
need to decide her major field of study.

Aga had already decided. "Economics is my best
subject. That's what I will study. What do you intend
to do when you grow up?"

Agnes thought about the question. Often adults
asked that question, and then smiled at the child's
simple-minded answer: "A lion tamer," "A river-
boat captain," "A rich and famous actress." Now
Agnes asked herself that question for real—and found
she had no answer.

The parish priest understood Agnes's problem. "As
a priest, one of my responsibilities is to help the boys
and girls to follow their vocation according to the call
of God."

"Vocation?" Agnes asked. "What do you mean?"

"Every person is the creation of God," explained
the priest. "When you give your life to His service,
He will fill your heart with a calling. You will have
an urge to undertake a certain kind of work—one for
which you are especially suited."

"Like missionary work?" Agnes asked.

The priest nodded. "Or teaching, or something else

of service to others. You must decide to follow your
own road according to the calling God has given you.''

"Missionary work does fascinate me," she said.
"Especially in India.''

The priest cautioned her. ''Mission work demands
more than fascination. It requires dedication,
sacrifices, and hard, lonely work.''

Agnes put the idea of missionary work out of her
mind—for a time.

The money problems of the Bojaxhiu household
grew less grim. Mother proved to have a good business
sense. She organized the neighborhood women into
the handicraft business. Week by week they gained
more customers.

Finally the day came when Dronda totaled the earn-
ings for the week and closed the account book with
satisfaction. ''We earned a profit this week for the first
time!'' she said in triumph.

Although the Bojaxhiu family could not be
described as well-to-do any more, quite clearly they
would not starve either.

''But I do become rather sick of rice and cabbage
every day,'' Aga admitted.

Agnes missed the good food, too. She'd always
brought a healthy appetite to the table. Until a year
ago, her brother kidded her about being plump.

''I may have been plump at one time. But not any
more!'' Agnes said. She learned to sew, not only to
make new dresses, but to mend her old ones.

Despite Dronda's success, she never became too
busy to help someone.

One day Agnes came home to find a cot set up in
the back room.

Dronda said, ''We'll have a woman living with us
for a time.''

''A boarder?'' Agnes asked. ''Will she pay rent?''

"No," answered Dronda. "This poor woman is sick. She has no one to help her. We'll offer her a home and care for her until she gets well."

Despite the hardships that helping the sick woman would bring, Agnes nodded. "The best way to forget your own problems is to help others with theirs," she repeated to herself.

As a young man in a house full of women, Lazar felt out of place. Two years after his father's sudden death, Lazar announced his plans to leave Skopje.

"I'll be attending the military academy in Albania," he said. He carried himself in a military manner and spoke with the cool confidence of a person sure of his own destiny.

After Lazar left, Agnes missed him more than she had thought she would. They differed in age by only two years, with Lazar the oldest. Then Aga graduated from high school. She took a full-time job at a store that sold ribbons, lace, and clothing trim.

Agnes overcame her loneliness by throwing herself into outside activities. She continued to tutor students at every opportunity. She played the accordion and mandolin, sang in the all-city choir, and was a featured soloist in the Albanian Church choir. She attended all of the church ceremonies.

A visit by Brother Anthony to Skopje renewed Agnes's interest in missionary work. Brother Anthony was the letter-writing Jesuit from India who reported on the work in Bengal. Agnes listened in complete attention as he described his adventures first hand.

Agnes asked Brother Anthony, "Is it possible for me to be meant for the life of a missionary?"

He gave her the same answer as the parish priest. "Wait for the confirmation of your vocation through prayer and meditation. Time, and God, will give you the answer."

But Agnes refused to take "no" for an answer. "Tell me how to go about becoming a missionary to India," she begged.

So Brother Anthony talked with the parish priest about Agnes.

"Brother Anthony," the priest said. "Agnes is an outstanding teacher. She enjoys teaching and cares about her students. But her nature is too tender to be thrust into the unspeakable poverty found throughout India."

Brother Anthony said, "I'll advise her to seek admission to the Congregation of the Loreto Nuns. The Loreto nuns are especially trained to be teachers. The schools they run in India are for the daughters of higher class British and Indian families."

"What a good idea!" the parish priest said. "If she is accepted, she will not come in contact with the poor people on the streets of India."

Brother Anthony spoke with Agnes before he left. "I suggest you apply to the Loreto congregation."

The priest assured her, "I'll help you seek admission to the Loreto congregation. Their headquarters is in Rathfranham, near Dublin, in Ireland."

"But I want to go to India, not Dublin," she protested.

"First you must learn to speak English and to write it," he told her.

"Then I can go to India?" Agnes asked.

"You can ask," Brother Anthony said. "I expect your superiors will agree. The Loreto Nuns have several schools in India. The schools were established years ago to teach the young girls of the leaders of the country."

The Irish nuns gave a positive reply to Agnes. "You are welcome to the postulate of the Sisters of Our Lady of Loreto in Ireland. There you will learn about being a Sister in our teaching order.''

So, seventeen-year-old Agnes Bojaxhiu made plans to leave Skopje and travel to Ireland to become a nun.

About this time, Lazar wrote home to announce that he'd been promoted to lieutenant. He was aghast to learn that Agnes intended to become a nun.

"How could you," he wrote, "a girl like you, become a nun? Do you realize that you are burying yourself?"

Agnes wrote back, "You think you are so important, as an official serving the king of two million subjects. Well, I'm an official, too, serving the King of the whole world. Which one of us is right?"

Lazar refused to accept the fact that his sister had become a nun. He resolved never to speak to her again. He didn't come home to see her off.

"Dear sweet Agnes, I'll carry your picture—but it will be the picture of the happy girl I used to know. I cannot—will not—picture you as a nun.''

When Agnes left for Ireland, she found all ties with Skopje cut. With Agnes leaving, Aga and Dronda decided to find a place in Albania to live.

"Yugoslavia is unstable," Aga said. "Mother and I will feel safer in Albania.''

Agnes wondered if she would ever see her birthplace again. Despite her quick reply to her brother's letter, a nagging doubt remained. Would her life come to nothing?

"There is no going back," Agnes said. "I will follow my own road.''

CALCUTTA

City of Palaces

The buildings of the Abby of Our Lady of Loreto stood old but beautiful on the sprawling estate in Ireland. White statues decorated carefully mowed lawns, while great curving walkways ran between the ancient brick buildings.

Agnes lived in a comfortable, well-worn dormitory. Thousands of other young girls had begun their lives as nuns here, and the wooden floors shone with their countless steps.

Agnes struggled to learn English. Because of the language barrier, she made few friends. Later, the other girls recalled little about her stay at the convent. They remembered her only as a shy, solitary person.

Agnes did make friends with Sister Xavier, a young nun who lived in the dormitory.

"I cannot imagine a place more different from my home in Skopje," Agnes admitted. "Even the weather surprises me. This morning I awoke to a cold fog. By midday bright sunlight made the lawns a dazzling green. And now, listen to the rain falling on the roof."

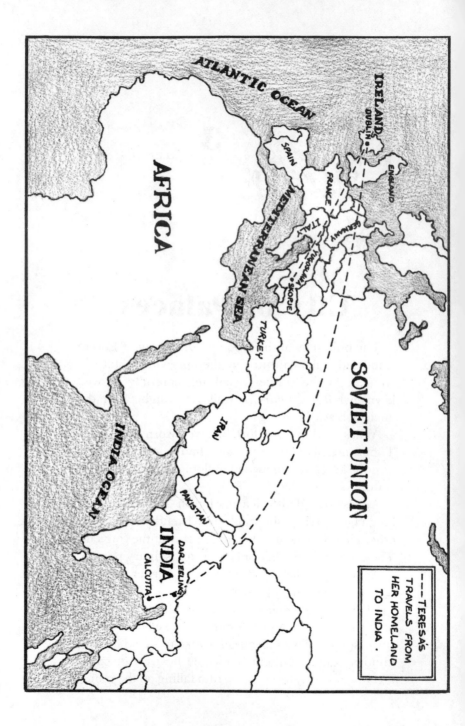

Sister Xavier agreed. "Ireland's weather can bring a tear and a smile in a single day."

Although she did not want to admit it, Agnes became terribly homesick. She learned the importance of prayer and putting her trust in God.

Her superiors took pity on the young girl who seemed so alone. "The reason for this first postulant year is to test and develop the young candidates for religious life," they said. "But that can be done as easily in India."

Because of this surprising and unexpected decision, Agnes lived at the Loreto Abby in Dublin, Ireland, for less than two months—from the end of November in 1928 to the first of January in 1929. Her superiors sent her directly from Rathfarnham to India.

"To Calcutta?" Agnes asked.

"No, to Darjeeling. You will teach in the Loreto convent there," her superiors explained. "Darjeeling is the summer resort town for the British in India. It is two hundred miles from Calcutta, in the cool foothills of the Himalaya Mountains. You'll find Darjeeling to be more nearly like your homeland than Rathfarnham."

"I did so want to see Calcutta," Agnes said wistfully.

"You will," they assured her. "The last part of your journey takes you by train through Calcutta."

But Agnes had little time for sightseeing when she arrived in Calcutta. She had to observe what she could of the city from the train windows.

"The City of Palaces," she said to herself. The British described Calcutta in that way, and with good reason.

The landmarks came into view as the train left Howrah Station and took her through the city— mansions of rich merchants, grand government

buildings, and Victorian palaces built on an extrava-
gant scale. The parks contained white marble
monuments to British rulers and heroes.

Calcutta had begun as a trading-post of the East
India Company. It grew into the most active shipping port in all Asia. The British built it into a major
city of the Empire, second only to London itself in
importance.

Calcutta could claim to be the most beautiful city
in India. Certainly it could boast to be the richest.
The city sported golf links, race courses, swimming
and riding clubs. Its museums contained great works
of art; its theater district presented new plays monthly;
its publishers printed more than a dozen literary
magazines. Students flocked to the city to attend the
university or to be trained at its medical center.

From 1771 to 1911 Calcutta served as the capital
of India. In 1911, when the British moved the capital
to Delhi, the change came as a terrible blow. For the
next twenty years Calcutta's population grew, but its
money and political power faded. The city became
overcrowded and uneasy about its future.

Here and there Agnes could see neglect and decay
taking over the proud buildings. Poor families lived
in the gardens of abandoned palaces and cooked over
open fires.

At her seat in the train Agnes sniffed the air and
wrinkled her nose. Calcutta smelled of incense, dust,
and smoke. It was the odor of too many people packed
too close together.

As the train gathered speed, Agnes put this unpleasant thought out of her mind. Sights of the countryside
flashed by the windows: mango orchards, palm
groves, tropical fields of rice, and ponds covered with
hyacinths.

The locomotive chugged louder when it started

uphill. The tracks twisted and turned, threading around towering mountains and through lush jungle valleys. At last it climbed more than a mile into the clouds and clattered to a stop at its destination, Darjeeling, the city of lightning.

Agnes stepped from the passenger car onto the platform. The train hissed and shot out a cloud of white steam. A crowd of people swept around, meeting friends and swarming over the freight cars to unload packages. Porters staggered under heavy loads; officials waved and blew whistles. Agnes looked around, uncertain of her direction.

A nun dressed in the black and white habit of Loreto came forward and took Agnes by the hand. An olive skinned Indian porter walked behind her.

"Welcome to Darjeeling," the nun said, hugging Agnes. "I am Mother Francis, headmistress of the school. Our man will carry your luggage. Is this one suitcase all you have?"

"Yes," Agnes said. "But I can carry it."

Mother Francis smiled. "The air is thin here," she said, "and the convent school is up there."

Agnes tilted her head back. An almost vertical flight of stairs led upward, into the misty heights. "I've never climbed stairs so steep or so high," Agnes admitted. She willingly let the porter take the luggage.

"Darjeeling perches on three levels along the side of the mountain," said Mother Francis. "The convent and school are on the top level."

As they climbed the stairs, Agnes saw narrow streets running left and right. Bazaars, marketplaces, small Indian hotels, and places to eat jammed against each other. Indians, Tibetans, and Nepalese—all colorful in their tribal clothing—lived and worked together.

"All of the races of India meet on the lower levels," said Mother Francis.

"And at the top?" Agnes asked.

"It's a private place for the governor of Bengal and the British, with the Indian servants who staff their villas. Each year government officials and well-off families escape the heavy, sticky heat of lower Bengal and Calcutta. They come here to enjoy our cool air and pleasant surroundings."

Agnes observed the nearly deserted streets on the top level. "It is so quiet."

"Tea time," Mother Francis explained. "All work stops for afternoon tea. Later, the shops will open."

They walked past the blue-domed government building, through the mall, and past elaborate hotels, European style cafes, and shops that sold fine clothing, delicate china, and carved ivory.

At the end of the way, they entered the gate to the stately grounds of Loreto Convent.

Once settled in at Darjeeling, Agnes threw herself into her language studies. Before the spring term began she could speak English fluently. Later she learned Bengali as well. She gladly took to her calling as a teacher of history and geography.

Healthy, well-scrubbed girls in perfectly matched uniforms attended the convent school.

After school, the girls enjoyed horseback riding along bridle paths, dressing up and promenading along the mall, dancing at the Gymkhana club, dining in fancy restaurants. They went on picnics overlooking the jungle where tigers, deer, and elephants roamed wild.

To the north the majestic Himalayas looked down, their dizzy peaks eternally capped in snow.

Agnes expressed her joy to the headmistress. "Everything is so rich, so pleasant, so beautiful! I'm indeed fortunate to live and work here."

Mother Francis cautioned her. "Life out there is

not as pleasant as inside our calm walls. The dark
clouds of a political storm are forming on India's
horizon. Last month, Mohandas Gandhi and his
Indian National Congress demanded an end to British
rule."

"But the British hold this country together," Agnes
protested.

"The Indians think otherwise," Mother Francis
told her. "The National Congress is on record as saying they will settle for nothing less than complete and
total freedom. They want India to be an independent
nation."

"Politics!" Agnes said, dismissing it from her mind.

She loved teaching and that is what concerned her.
Her students responded to her love with affection and
respect.

On May 24, 1931, Agnes Gonxha Bojaxhiu took
her first vows as a nun. She elected the name Teresa,
a choice inspired by St. Theresa of Lisieux, who had
lived from 1873-1897, the French nun known as the
"Little Flower of Jesus."

Agnes donned the long black gown and white head
covering of the Loreto nuns.

"God willed it," Agnes, now Sister Teresa, wrote
to her mother. "He made the choice."

Mail sent to her mother and sister suffered delay
and interference because of the communist government of Albania. Agnes learned to send her letters
to a friend in Italy. He carried them in person to her
Mother and Aga when he traveled to Albania on
business trips.

Agnes wrote to her brother Lazar, too, but he didn't
answer her letters.

After taking her first vows, Sister Teresa received
a call to come to Calcutta. The call came from Mother

de Senacle, the principal of the Loreto school at
Entally.

"We would like for you to teach at Saint Mary's
High School," Mother de Senacle explained. "Saint
Mary's is for Bengali girls. The girls, who are from
good families, are taught in their own language."

Sister Teresa left Darjeeling after two years to accept
the teaching post in Calcutta. The Entally district was
on the eastern side of Calcutta. Although in a poor
neighborhood, the Loreto nuns occupied a spacious
property provided by a wealthy Protestant planter.
Saint Mary's High School for Girls shared grounds
with the convent.

At Entally, Sister Teresa set her whole heart to the
education of the Bengali girls.

Six years later, on May 24, 1937, Sister Teresa took
her final vows.

Sister Teresa became the headmistress of Saint
Mary's. She also looked after the Daughters of Saint
Anne, an Indian religious order attached to the Loreto
sisters.

Sister Teresa lived a comfortable, although unevent-
ful life. During the next ten years she came to feel
completely at home in India.

Of course, not everything was sweetness and light.
Outside the protective walls of Entally, Calcutta's
poverty grew more serious. The poor of India flocked
to Calcutta to look for a better life. Most failed to find
work. Instead, they became homeless. They lived in
decaying buildings or even along the sidewalks.

The high walls of the convent set it apart as an oasis
of tranquility in the midst of the misery.

Once Mother de Senacle tried an experiment to help
some of the unfortunate children of the streets. She
took in twenty girls from the slum and appointed a
Sister to feed, dress, wash, and teach them.

After a year, only two girls remained.

"What happened?" Teresa asked. "Why did the others leave?"

Mother de Senacle shook her head sadly. "We tried to make them feel at home. But the girls never became comfortable here. Poor people need a school of their own."

The resources of the city could not overcome the suffering and squalor. People who visited Calcutta threw up their hands in dismay. "Conditions in the city cannot become any more dreadful."

Yet, incredibly, conditions did grow worse.

In 1947, India became free. To satisfy conflicts between Moslems and Hindus, Bengal was divided and part of it became East Pakistan. Millions of Hindu refugees streamed into the already over-populated city.

The Hindu students at St. Mary's looked about for good works they could do. One of Teresa's students, Subhasini Das, led the girls.

Although a small girl, bright-eyed and shy, Subhasini Das displayed an incredible strength of character. Another student, Magdalene Gomes, helped. She possessed a sharp mind combined with a sense of humor and the ability to deal with others.

Subhasini Das, Magdalene Gomes, and the other girls organized a visit every week to sick people at Nilratan Sarkar Hospital. They consoled the patients, wrote letters for them, and performed other small services.

The girls grew enthusiastic about their volunteer work and decided to invite Teresa to accompany them.

"Sister Teresa," Subhasini Das said, "will you come with us this week?"

Teresa hesitated. "My work is here," she said.

As she spoke she saw the disappointment on their

faces. The girls looked up to her. They respected her. To refuse would dampen their spirits.

"Yes," she agreed quickly. "I'll go with you."

Teresa stepped out of the convent into a nightmare.

On the way they passed through one of the slums. She saw unwashed children in tattered clothing. The children looked out at the world with the sunken eyes of those who missed too many meals. The sick and weary lay on the sidewalk or slumped in doorways. Vultures hovered around, patiently waiting.

The hospital swarmed with people—nurses, doctors, the sick who lay everywhere, even in the halls. The nurses tried to make their rounds, but could find time only for the worst cases.

An old man lying on a cot smiled in thanks as the girls from Saint Mary's washed the mud from his body.

"He fell in a drain and stayed there all night" the nurse said. "His leg is broken."

"And the baby?" Teresa asked, looking at a baby whose leg was wrapped in bandages.

"Rats," the nurse explained to her. "During the night rats ate his foot. He was too weak from hunger to cry out."

They saw patients feverish with diseases such as typhoid and malaria. Others suffered broken bones and infection. A few came in with ailments seen nowhere else in the world.

Teresa drew back from the suffering. The horror of the hospital repelled her. With relief she welcomed the safety and comfort of the convent.

"I'll let Subhasini Das and Magdalene Gomes and the other girls carry on with the good works outside the convent walls," she resolved. She planned to devote herself to teaching, and only to teaching.

But the Lord she served had other plans for her.

CALCUTTA

City of Dreadful Night

Late on the afternoon of September 10, 1946, Teresa left the Loreto Convent in Entally for Howrah Station. She boarded the train to take her to a religious retreat in Darjeeling.

Rudyard Kipling, author of the Jungle Books, described Calcutta as "The City of Dreadful Night." As the gloom of late afternoon lengthened, the city earned that title. Dilapidated tram cars rattled noisily along potholed streets. The unemployed and destitute lay with their backs to the decaying buildings. Stray dogs snarled and barked.

Although Calcutta had been a beautiful city, decay and poverty caused much of it to be called the ugliest city in India. Certainly it was the poorest. A half million people called the sidewalks and alleys their homes. They were born on the streets, lived on the streets, and fully expected to die on the streets.

The train station supported its share of the homeless. They bedded down for the night in any likely spot—on the platform, on the steps, and on the concrete floors along the hall.

Fifteen years earlier, when Teresa came to Calcutta as the young and inexperienced Agnes Bojaxhiu, she failed to see—really see—the poverty of Calcutta.

Now the poor people thrust themselves upon her. She tried to ignore their desperate condition, but failed.

At every stop along the way, beggers thrust their hands through the train windows. "Baksheesh! Baksheesh!" they cried, begging for alms, or money. "No father, no mother, no family. Give money!"

As the journey to Darjeeling continued, Agnes tried to sleep. The train wheels, hammering out a mournful sound on the tracks, kept time with her troubled thoughts. Teresa prayed about what she had seen that day. As she did, the voice of Jesus acted upon her heart.

"You must do something."

"Yes, Lord," Teresa answered. "But what?"

"Thou shalt love the Lord thy God with thy whole heart, and with thy whole soul, and with thy whole mind."

"Yes," Teresa said. "I do love You."

"I was hungry and you gave Me no food; I was thirsty and you gave Me no drink; I was a stranger and you did not take Me in, naked and you did not clothe Me, sick and in prison and you did not visit Me."

"Oh, Lord, when did I see You hungry and sick? When did I not minister to You?"

"I say to you, inasmuch as you did not do it to one of the least of these, you did not do it to Me."

Teresa called this her "Day of Decision." The message was quite clear. She was to leave the convent and help poor people while living among them.

After returning from the religious retreat in Darjeeling, Teresa went to see the Archbishop of Calcutta.

Archbishop Ferdinand Perier, a gentleman eighty years old, listened patiently.

Teresa pleaded her case. "I have a second call. The message I heard on the train is to give up Loreto and go out on the streets. I am to serve Christ in the slums among the poorest of the poor."

"Why do you feel so strongly about this?" the Archbishop asked.

Teresa plunged ahead, "Because I see those people for what they are—Christ in disguise. He is the hungry man, the lonely woman, the homeless boy, the little girl seeking shelter. It is the hungry Christ that I will feed, it is the naked Christ I will clothe, it is for the homeless Christ I will find shelter."

"Your plans will require you to leave the Loreto nuns," Archbishop Perier pointed out.

He thought for a time, then he gave his decision. "I must refuse your request. Nuns who have taken final vows are not permitted to leave the convent. I cannot grant you permission to leave your order."

Teresa accepted the Archbishop's decision. She could not do otherwise. She returned to Entally to teach. Now, however, she also put herself into the work of visiting the poor and sick.

Father Henry, a humble and practical man, worked with the boys at his church and with the girls of St. Mary's in planning their weekly trips into the slums.

Teresa told Father Henry about her day of decision aboard the train. "I asked the Archbishop to allow me to live among the poor," she said. "But he refused."

Father Henry understood. "There was nothing else he could have said. He cannot give permission to start a new order to the first nun who comes along, even if you do say God has asked it of you."

"I must help in whatever way I can," she said. "What is the worst slum in the entire city?"

"Moti Jheel, I suppose," answered Father Henry.

"Where is Moti Jheel?" Teresa asked.

"Right here," Father Henry said. "You can see it from the porch. Moti Jheel is just on the other side of the convent walls." Moti Jheel didn't look anything like what it's name implied—Pearl Lake.

Teresa stood on the porch and looked over the convent wall. At first she saw only tin roofs and narrow lanes. On closer inspection she saw the garbage-littered streets, mud houses and lean-tos thrown up against available walls, and people everywhere. The people of Moti Jheel moved in and out of their little one-room houses like bees swarming around a beehive.

Teresa shook her head. "How blind I have been!" she said sadly. "For fifteen years I've lived next to

this shantytown filled with disease and misery. Yet, only now am I disturbed by what I see.''

Teresa walked each week with her girls into the bustees, or shantytowns.

For two years Father Henry, Teresa, and the girls of St. Mary's made their weekly trips into the slums and to the hospitals.

''Instead of dreading the trips to the poor,'' Teresa told Father Henry, ''I look forward to them. With every day I am becoming more certain of the rightness of my desire to leave Loreto.''

Father could find little to encourage her. ''You are a European. With independence in the air, you may expect to be opposed by the local people.''

Father Henry saw the stubborn look on her face. ''On the other hand,'' he added quickly, ''if your work is needed, then God will bless it.''

For the second time Teresa appealed to Archbishop Perier. ''Living at the convent is like being on an island of plenty while a great ocean of misery and despair is before me. God wants me as an uncloistered nun, living with the poor.''

Archbishop Perier looked at this frail woman more closely. She stood hardly more than five feet tall and weighed less than one hundred pounds. But those blue-gray eyes burned bright and clear, the eyes of a person absolutely determined to serve the Lord in the way she felt He directed.

This time he could not turn her down outright. ''First, seek permission of the Mother General of the Loreto nuns. If she grants permission, then come back to me. I will help you draft a letter to the Pope.''

Mother Gertrude, Mother General of the congregation in Rathfranham, wrote back promptly. ''If God is calling you, I give you permission with all my heart. I want you to know that we love you, and if you ever

want to come back to us, there will always be a place
for you.''

With the help of Archbishop Perier, Teresa wrote
to Pope Pius XII. They mailed the letter to Rome on
February 2, 1948. Teresa requested that she "live
alone outside the cloister among the poor of Calcutta,
with God alone as protector and guide.''

Archbishop Perier warned her, "The letter is not
a simple formality. Rome always hesitates to authorize
a new congregation. Too often such a move begins
strong—and then fades out.''

On April 12, 1948, Pius XII gave Teresa permission to leave the Loreto Convent. But for the new
order to come into existence, ten novices would have
to join her during the next two years.

"I think the poor will accept me," Teresa told
Father Henry. "I will live among them, dress as they
do, and eat the same food they eat. I already feel
myself to be at home in India, so I have begun making plans to become an Indian citizen.''

The Loreto habit that she wore, however, would
never do. Its stark black and white stood out too much.
"I will have to design new clothes, more in keeping
with Indian customs," she decided.

But for right now she faced a difficult chore: leaving Loreto in which she had been so happy.

She told Mother de Senacle, "Leaving Loreto is
the greatest sacrifice, the most difficult thing I have
ever done. It is a lot more difficult than leaving my
family and country to become a nun. Loreto has been
everything to me.''

"What are your immediate plans?" Mother de
Senacle asked.

"Medical training," Teresa answered promptly.
"So many poor people suffer from terrible diseases
such as typhoid, malaria, cholera, and smallpox.

Practical training in hygiene will let me show them how to stay healthy.''

"Medical training?" Mother de Senacle wondered aloud. "Doesn't that require a long time?"

"Usually it does," Teresa agreed. "But in my case the Medical Missionary Sisters in Patna are offering a special speeded-up course."

For three months, Teresa lived in Patna, a city three hundred miles from Calcutta. At Patna, on the right bank of the Ganges, the American Medical Missionary Sisters ran a hospital and nurses' training course.

Mother Dengel directed the school. Like Teresa, Mother Dengel possessed an incredible amount of energy and force of will. She succeeded in getting permission for her nuns to perform surgery, something new for her time.

More than anyone else, Mother Dengel understood Teresa and what Teresa hoped to do.

Teresa described her plans to Mother Dengel. "We—myself and the good sisters who work with me—will preach Christ to the poor, not only in words, but in day-by-day living."

Mother Dengel said, "It will mean a congregation entirely devoted to this work."

"Yes, you do see what I mean," Teresa said. "We will wear the same clothes, possess as little, live as humbly, and eat no more than the poorest of the poor. We will eat rice and nothing else."

Mother Dengel held up her hands, "I must disagree. You need to eat well. The very poor work only a little. But even so, they grow weak, become sick, and die. You will work long, hard hours each day. You will be among the sick in unhealthy surroundings."

"I didn't see our diet to be that important," Teresa admitted.

"You must consider it wisely," Mother Dengel said. "Good food is essential for good health."

Teresa accepted Mother Dengel's advice. She changed her plans. "Sisters who work with me will be given simple food—but adequate portions. I'll see to it they eat everything set before them."

While undertaking the medical training, Teresa planned her new habit and wore it for the first time. For four rupees she bought a white cotton sari with a blue border. In her sari she would be wearing the common dress of Indian women. She used a large safety pin to hold a cross to the left shoulder of the sari.

The nurses at Patna Holy Family Hospital completed the new habit. They presented Teresa with a pair of sandals.

Teresa met Miss Jacqueline de Decker, a patient at the hospital.

"I wish I could work with you," Jacqueline said. "I came to India two years ago as a missionary. But now my work must end before it has really begun."

She explained, "I will soon leave India to return to Belgium to undergo an operation. But. . .the surgeons offer little hope of improving my condition."

Teresa could see that the young lady suffered pain all the time. Yet Jacqueline smiled and encouraged others despite the hopelessness of her own condition. Time and again Teresa visited Jacqueline and came away cheered by the young woman's example.

Before Teresa left Patna she made a proposal to Jacqueline. "You can have a part of the work," Teresa said. "Offer your prayers for me. Your spiritual support and prayers for success will give meaning to my work."

Jacqueline quickly agreed. Not only did she pray,

but she wrote to others in the same condition as herself. They put Teresa's work in their prayers, too.

Later, regardless of the problems, Teresa took comfort in knowing that somewhere in the world people prayed daily for her.

Teresa, wearing her new habit, returned to Calcutta on Christmas Eve.

"Do you recognize me?" Teresa asked Father Henry.

Father Henry said, "Of course. Have you found a place to live yet?"

"No," Teresa said. "I am staying with the Little Sisters of the Poor. I will look for a room tomorrow."

She left the next morning, carrying bread for the poor, some medicine, and soap to wash the sick.

That evening she walked back more exhausted than any other time in her life.

She stopped to talk with Father Henry at his church. "Today I learned a great lesson," she reported. "The poverty of the poor must be so hard for them. When looking for a home, I walked and walked until my legs and arms ached. I thought how much they must ache in soul and body looking for a home, food, and health."

"Must you do this?" Father Henry asked. "Loreto will welcome you back."

"What you say is a terrible temptation," Teresa admitted. "As I walked back so worn out I thought about Loreto convent. A regular life with its security and protection is a strong attraction."

"Stay in tomorrow and rest," Father Henry suggested.

"No," Teresa said. "I must go back out."

The next day Teresa again set out hunting for a place to live. But her legs refused to carry her.

She prayed, "My God, I love You, and I choose

freely to remain faithful to my decision to do only Your work.''

Rather than leave the slums in despair, Teresa turned to what she knew best—teaching.

She found five street children, children without a family. She brought them to a public park. There she began her first school. Her classroom had no tables, no chairs, and no blackboard. She flattened out a patch of ground with her hand and started writing with a stick.

She remembered the questions the girls of St. Mary's answered, questions such as: Describe the theme of the poem, ''The Lady of Shallot,'' and explain its meaning.

These children needed to learn more basic ideas! Although older, they'd never been to school. She began by teaching them the Bengali alphabet and the rules of hygiene.

She showed them how to wash with water and a bar of soap. Some of the students had never seen soap. It was a luxury far beyond their dreams.

When she finished the day's lessons she found herself refreshed. With renewed strength she visited poor families in the area. She asked about their needs.

''I'll be back tomorrow,'' she told them.

The next day, to her amazement, twenty-three children came to her open-air classroom. Someone found a broken blackboard and donated it to the ''school.''

She began classes by washing the children. As she did, she saw how much they suffered from too little food. Nor could she overlook their tattered clothing.

That night she walked to the homes of the rich families who sent their children to St. Mary's. She explained her new work and asked for their help.

"Help the poor?" one Hindu woman said. "The poor do not ask for help."

"They starve in silence. If they die it is not because God doesn't care for them, but because you and I don't give. We are the tools of love in the hands of God. Give them bread, give them clothing, help heal them and teach them. You'll be helping Christ."

The appeal fell on deaf ears.

On the third day, forty-one students came. The people of the slum found her a tiny shed covered with a tin roof. They even found a battered table.

After a week or so, Father Henry came to visit. Teresa showed him around.

"How many pupils do you have?" he asked.

"From thirty to fifty," she said. "They are never all here at once. Some are sick or absent for one reason or another. I give them a bar of soap as a prize for not missing."

Father Henry, always a kindly man, tried to show enthusiasm for her work. But he could not be impressed. The whole thing seemed so pitiful, thirty slum children out of a population of more than five million!

He looked around the place. The silence grew more painful.

"It's not much," she said lamely.

Father Henry changed the subject. "Have you found a home yet?"

"No," Teresa said. "I still stay with the Little Sisters of the Poor at their home for aged persons."

He left her to her bleak thoughts. She had no food, no funds, no prospect of even finding a home for herself. What chance did she really have to bring hope to Calcutta's poor, especially since she worked alone? Would someone come forward to help her with the work?

CALCUTTA

5

Creek Lane

In February of 1949, Father Henry came to Teresa
with good news. "A room is for rent on Creek Lane,"
he said.

"Creek Lane?" Teresa said doubtfully. "That area
is much too good. I want something more humble."

"Please don't reject it out of hand," Father Henry
said. "Creek Lane is centrally located, only a few
blocks from Nilratan Sarkar Hospital, and you can
walk to the slums from there."

"Whose house is it?" Teresa asked.

"Michael Gomes," Father Henry said. "His three
brothers used to live with him. But a few months
before the division of India, two of the brothers
decided to go to East Pakistan. They are Christians,
and they felt a calling to help other Christians in the
new country. The whole top floor of the Gomes home
is empty."

"But I need only one room, not an entire floor."

"Go talk to Mr. Gomes," Father Henry suggested.
Teresa took Father Henry's advice.

The houses stood majestic, but tired, along Creek
Lane. Old lamp posts once burned gas for light. Now
the posts had been wired for electricity. Creeping vines
overran walls that protected rambling three-story
homes. White columns held up sagging porches. The
whole area looked neglected and worn.

Teresa passed a mansion with an iron gate. Outside the gate, plaster lions stood watch beside a guard's
empty station. Tall trees crowded along the way,
casting the sidewalk in dark shadows.

Teresa came to 14 Creek Lane, the Gomes home,
and knocked at the door of the old-fashioned building.

Michael Gomes answered. He was a slim man,
wearing glasses. His calm speech perfectly matched
the quiet and reserved neighborhood in which he lived.

Teresa introduced herself. ''I understand you have
a room to rent?''

''Yes,'' he said. ''Come, let me show it to you.''

He took her around to the side. "From the ground floor a staircase leads directly to the top floor."

As her eyes adjusted to the gloom, Teresa made out a wide hallway opening into several large rooms. Boxes of all sizes stood at odd angles on the floor, their surfaces covered with dust.

"There are five rooms here. As you can see, my brothers left their furniture behind. But we can move it out and make one room for you to use."

"How much is the rent?" Teresa asked.

"Five rupees a month," Michael Gomes answered.

"I'll take it," Teresa said.

The next day Teresa moved into her new home. She brought a suitcase, a chair, and an empty packing case for a desk.

"When will the rest of your things be delivered?" Michael Gomes asked.

"This is it," Teresa said.

He could not let Teresa begin with such a bleakly furnished room. "Pick out what you like from the other furniture," he said.

Teresa, however, rejoiced at having a room of her own. Now she could work without disturbing others. In addition to her long hours during the day, Teresa began staying up late at night. She sat at the packing crate desk and wrote letters—hundreds of letters. She wrote to former students, to their families, and to the well-to-do friends from her days at St. Mary's. She told about her work and asked for their help.

No one came forward to join her. The entire community she hoped to establish still consisted of only one person: herself.

The generosity of Michael Gomes and his wife brightened those long days. They gave her hope. Surely, somewhere in Calcutta lived others with kind hearts and generous natures like that of this Christian family. When it came time for Teresa to pay her rent, Michael Gomes turned it down.

"I count it a great honor to have you share my home," he said. "You do the work of God, and you will be treated as an honored guest." In all the time Teresa lived at 14 Creek Lane, Michael Gomes never accepted any money for the services he provided.

"You are a most holy man," she said.

In the spring of 1949, Subhasini Das, the former student from St. Mary's, came to visit. Subhasini flashed a smile. The girl, from a good family, wore an expensive sari. She looked so alive, so healthy, compared to the weak and sick people Teresa met every day.

Subhasini said, "I want to become one of your sisters."

Teresa's heart skipped a beat. Subhasini possessed all of the qualities Teresa wanted in a recruit—good humor, intelligence, a charming personality, a healthy body, and a firm Christian faith. Subhasini radiated love and compassion. Could anyone be more suited for the work among the poorest of the poor?

At last Teresa said, "You are young and beautiful. If you join me, you'll have to give up everything, even yourself. Your life will be a long one of self-denial."

"Sister Teresa," Subhasini said, "I have known you since I was nine years old. You inspired me. I am prepared for the work."

To her surprise, Teresa found herself uncomfortable. Now she understood how the parish priest back in Skopje must have felt. To encourage a young and inexperienced girl to undertake such an awesome task put great responsibility upon Teresa's shoulders. If Subhasini failed, then Teresa would share in that failure.

Teresa borrowed a technique she'd learned from

Archbishop Perier—delay. Only by throwing a gentle roadblock before Subhasini could she be certain that the girl was serious.

"Subhasini," Teresa said, "go home and think about your decision for a few days. This must not be a passing fancy, but a lifelong choice. If you still feel the same, then see me again on Saint Joseph's day."

Turning the girl away took almost more courage than Teresa could muster. But she felt it was the right approach.

On March 19, 1949, Subhasini Das did come back. The young Bengali wore a white sari of coarse cloth with a blue border, and a cross at the shoulder.

"I have come to stay," Subhasini said.

Within a few days Magdalene Gomes joined them. One by one other girls from Saint Mary's knocked on the door at 14 Creek Lane. They came to serve the poorest of the poor, too.

Teresa prayed, "Thank You, Lord Jesus. How good You are! Keep sending them!"

Teresa and her girls took over more and more of the top floor. Now it began to look like a convent. When the number grew to ten, Teresa began thinking about rules for her new order. A formal constitution would have to be written for the congregation to be officially recognized.

"Our congregation will be called the Missionary Sisters of Charity," she decided. "The girls will take the usual three vows of poverty, chastity, and obedience. But there will be a fourth one: To serve the poorest of the poor."

The rich began to help. Mrs. Chater, a Chinese woman, owned a car and could find her way through the confusing tangle of streets. She came each day to drive the girls to faraway places in Calcutta.

The daily activity of the girls fell into a pattern.

At 4:30 A.M. they awoke for prayers and meditation. "Prayer gives us the love and strength to make
the suffering people feel better," Teresa explained.
The prayers lasted until breakfast at half past six.
Before leaving for the day, the girls washed their
clothes and mopped the floors.

"Washing vigorously is essential," Teresa told
them. "Each day you come in contact with infectious
diseases. Boil your clothes. Scrub the floors. Kill those
germs!"

By 8:00 A.M. they walked off in pairs to their
various outside duties—some to the slum schools in
Moti Jheel, others to clinics, some to help the old and
weak. A few took the crowded tram cars to other parts
of the city.

When children heard Sister Teresa and her girls
coming, they would skip ahead to meet them, smiling and singing.

The generosity of poor people amazed Teresa. One
day she learned about a Hindu family with eight
children who had not eaten for many days. Teresa
and Subhasini took a small bag of rice to the family.

When she stepped inside the tiny one-room house
with its dirt floor, her heart went out to what she saw.
The children's ribs protruded. She took in her arms
a baby who looked at her with large round eyes. It
had arms and legs as thin as a pencil.

Teresa spoke in a low voice to Subhasini, "This
is what real hunger looks like."

Subhasini gave the bag of rice to the grateful
mother. "This is for you and your children,"
Subhasini said.

The mother carefully divided the rice into two equal
parts. She wrapped one part in a napkin and left the
house. She came back empty handed.

"Where is the rice you took with you?" Teresa asked.

The woman said, "My neighbor is hungry also."

This Hindu woman had given half the rice to the next-door neighbors, a Moslem family.

"It takes courage and love to share like that," Teresa said.

At noon the girls came home for lunch. They ate cheap food, but plenty of it. The two most important foods were rice and bulgur. Bulgur, a crude wheat mash, looked unappetizing when cooked. But the staple came in generous amounts from America.

Teresa piled their plates high with rice and the bulgur. A new girl would look at the plate with astonishment.

"Eat it," Teresa would say. "God wants girls who can serve, not victims of malnutrition."

One of the girls confided to Subhasini. "What am I to do?" she asked. "I cannot eat what is put on my plate."

"Yes," another girl said. "With so many people going hungry, shouldn't we eat less?"

"I'll talk to Sister Teresa," Subhasini said.

The next day they had their answer—Teresa served even larger amounts.

"The question of serving sizes has been decided," Teresa said. "You will eat everything put before you in obedience."

Eventually the girls developed a taste for the bulgur. They benefited from it in other ways. The bags it came in could be used to make shirts, bedspreads, and bandages.

Subhasini said, "Perhaps the next postulant should take the name 'Sister Bulgur' in honor of this useful donation from the American people."

After the noon meal, younger girls stayed at the

convent to study. Four of them still attended high school, the youngest being only fifteen years old. The girls did their school work, studied the Bible, and listened to classes in religion.

Even after they finished high school, Teresa encouraged her girls to attend special schools and colleges.

"We need a doctor badly," Teresa said. "Magdalene, you should aim for that work."

"They'll never accept me," Magdalene said. "I haven't enough hours in math."

"You'll pass the test," Teresa assured her. "I'll coach you."

The crash course succeeded. The medical school accepted Magdalene into their program.

Teresa and her girls worked hard, they studied hard, and they played hard, too. After dinner, they filled the terrace on the upper floor with laughter and singing. Their tug-of-wars and hopscotch made the whole house shake. Then, as it grew dark, a bell rang to call them inside.

Teresa spoke to them, explaining the purpose of the Missionary Sisters of Charity. "We are first of all Christians. We are not social workers. We serve Jesus, who comes in the form of poor people. We nurse Him, feed Him, clothe Him, visit Him, and comfort Him. We do it all for Jesus. Let kindness be in your face, in your smile, in the warmth of your greeting. Never think in terms of a crowd, only of one person. Finally, treat the poor alike whether they be Hindu, Christian, or Moslem. Yes, treat them all the same. We are not neutral concerning our religion; let your lives preach Christ."

After Teresa became an Indian citizen in 1948, government agencies were more willing to help her in caring for orphans.

She told Michael Gomes, "The government is

giving me thirty-three rupees to spend on each child. Isn't that wonderful?''

Michael Gomes worked for the government. He saw problems with the program. ''The government closely oversees the money they give out. You'll have to keep records, meet with a committee twice a month, and follow their rules.''

''I can do that,'' Teresa said.

Six months later, she admitted to him it had been a mistake. ''You were right. They wanted me to spend 33 rupees on the children in the program. But I spend only 17 rupees on our other children. Is that fair? Today I told them to keep their money.''

On October 7, 1950, Rome approved the new congregation. Archbishop Perier came to celebrate Mass in their convent in the Gomes home.

Father Henry and the boys from his church converted the landing at the top of the stairs into a chapel. They furnished it with a wooden altar and wooden candlestick holders.

Subhasini Das made her vows and took the name Sister Agnes. She took the name in honor of Teresa, of course. Magdalene Gomes took the name Sister Gertrude. The congregation grew: Sister Frederick, Sister Dorothy, Sister Margaret, Sister Mary, Sister Eugene. More than 25 sisters lived at 14 Creek Lane.

Teresa—now Mother Teresa—and the Missionary Sisters of Charity occupied the entire top floor, as well as part of another building. Father Henry and his boys came around to help put in more showers and to move partitions. But no way they arranged it would give enough room for the growing congregation.

One day a Sister got chicken-pox. Teresa put her in a room to herself. This made the crowding in the other rooms worse.

''We need more room,'' Teresa told Father Henry.

"Not only for ourselves, but room for the sick, the dying, the homeless, the orphans, the babies too small and too weak to care for themselves." But she didn't know where she could find the extra space.

Mother Teresa tried to provide her workers with whatever they required. A young doctor gave his time to look at sick people. He wrote out some prescriptions for the medicines they needed.

She showed the long list to Michael Gomes.

"But where will you get the medicines?" Michael Gomes asked.

"I don't know," Teresa admitted. "But find them I must, not only for the poor, but so this good doctor will help us again. Any suggestions?"

"I know of a place," he said. "I've never been there, but I have talked to the man on the telephone."

"Good!" Teresa said. "Take me there."

They left in a driving downpour of rain. The

streetcar took them near the large shop that sold the medicine. Teresa and Michael Gomes rushed through the rain to the door.

Along the way they passed one of the street people. He huddled under a bench, trying to keep the rain off with newspaper.

At the medicine shop, she presented the manager with the list of drugs.

"This is a large order," he said. "Come back in two days and I'll have it ready."

"We'll wait," Teresa said.

The manager said, "Filling the order will take some time. It will be expensive, too."

"We have the time," Teresa said.

"And the money?" the manager asked.

"Can you let us have this at a big discount?" Teresa asked. She tapped the list with her finger.

"How big?" the manager asked.

"Free," Teresa answered.

The man stepped back, as if afraid of the little woman before him.

"You've come to the wrong place!" he said, and stalked away.

Teresa left the list on the counter. She sat down with her head bowed in prayer.

Two hours passed.

The manager returned, carrying five parcels. "All right, here is your complete order. You may have them as a gift from the company."

She smiled and nodded.

Outside, the slow, heavy rain continued to fall.

Mother Teresa stopped by the bench. She spoke to the man covered by the soggy newspaper. He didn't answer. She kneeled down and pulled back the newspaper. Raindrops fell across the man's face. He did not move.

She touched the man's cheek. His cold flesh told the story. "He's dead," she exclaimed.

"Mother," Michael Gomes said gently, "There is nothing you can do." He took her arm.

She stood up, numb at the sight of the dead beggar.

As she rode home that afternoon her mind kept coming back to the dead beggar. "To think," she said, "he died in the rain, all alone."

Place of the Pure Heart

Each morning when garbage collectors of Calcutta made their rounds they faced a grisly task. On the average they carted away the bodies of thirty people who died on the streets during the night. Like the beggar in the rain, these street people died alone and without anyone to care for them.

One morning shortly after finding the beggar, Teresa walked from the Gomes home to the Nilratan Sarkar Hospital. Along the way she saw in an alley a heap of rags gathered around the still form of a woman's body.

Teresa walked closer. Large rats looked up at her with beady eyes. Reluctantly, they scurried away.

Teresa brushed aside the sackcloth. She pulled in her breath, shocked at the awful sight. Rats had gnawed away the woman's feet. Ants and other insects crawled on festering sores all over her body. The smell of death became almost overpowering.

Yet, despite her condition, the woman still breathed. She lived! Incredible!

"How did she survive the night?" Teresa wondered. Then, a more horrible thought struck her. The woman could not have crawled into the alley by herself. Someone carried her here and left her in the trash to die. "People look after a dog or a cat better than this. They would not allow this to happen to their pets."

Teresa picked up the woman and carried her to the hospital.

When the nurse saw the sad bundle of rags, she began shaking her head. "This woman cannot be admitted," the nurse said.

"Please make room for her," Teresa said. "She is an emergency case."

The nurse waved her hand in the air, a gesture of dismissal. "We must let in only those we can help. There is no hope for her. She is going to die anyway. We have no room for hopeless cases."

Teresa was aghast. She asked, "Do you want me to take her back outside to die on the street?" Teresa refused to move.

When the nurse saw that Teresa would not leave, she took the woman, but only to avoid a bad scene.

As Teresa waited, she saw the hospital turn others away, especially poor and dying people. To be in pain, destitute, without friends is pathetic. But to die in anguish and despair on the streets must be the most cruel blow of all!

What Calcutta needed, she decided, was a place for the dying to spend their last hours. These dying destitutes should have a home to welcome them with love, consideration, and dignity.

Before leaving the hospital, Teresa received word about the woman from the alley. As the nurse predicted, the woman died within a couple of hours.

Teresa left the hospital and went immediately to

Dr. Ahmed, the Health Officer of the Calcutta Corporation. The Corporation was the governing body of the city of Calcutta.

Dr. Ahmed leaned back in his chair and listened. She told him, "It is a shame for a civilized city to have people die on its streets. Give me a place where the poor can die with dignity and love."

"You want a hospital?" he asked, puzzled. "A clinic? A place to feed the poor?"

She explained, "Give me a place in the city and I will take in dying destitutes who are turned away by hospitals. Yes, we will feed them and give them what medical attention we can. But the place will be for the dying who have nowhere else to go."

Such an unusual request, Dr. Ahmed thought. "I do know of a place," he said. "Near the temple of the goddess Kali is a large building. Originally, travelers from distant places who came to worship at the temple stayed there overnight. It is empty now and not being used for anything."

"That might do," Teresa said.

The health officer did not tell the complete story. The building was supposed to be empty. But thieves, drug addicts, gamblers, and gangs of youths used the building as a meeting place. On several occasions the police had cleared out the place. But the undesirables always drifted back in and took it over again.

"Let me show it to you," Dr. Ahmed said. If she took the place, then she would have to deal with the thieves and vandals.

The Darmashalah, or Pilgrim's Hotel, stood next door to the temple of the goodess Kali. Kali, the Hindu goddess of death and destruction, was Calcutta's most powerful deity. Hindus built the temple to her in 1809.

Rich and poor of all castes came to worship Kali.

The statue showed Kali with four arms. It was pure black except for a red tongue that hung down to her chest. Her faithful worshipers offered expensive gifts to this brooding statue of death. They stacked so many flowers before her that by the end of the day only her tongue showed.

About four hundred monks attended to the goddess and the temple.

Because of the tourists and pilgrims, shops in the area did a good business. The shops sold ivory, images, flowers, and gifts.

Street vendors called out their wares: balloons, brightly colored birds, fresh fish, and toys for children. Monkeys chattered and performed tricks. Snake charmers played flutes, causing cobras to weave out of wicker baskets. Beggars held out their hands and cried for alms.

Dr. Ahmed showed Teresa through the Pilgrim's Hotel. Although large, the building contained only two rooms. Small windows of colored glass set high in the wall filtered out most of the light.

"It's rather gloomy," Teresa said.

"The city whitewashed the outside recently," Dr. Ahmed pointed out, anxious for her to take the building.

They stepped from the gray interior back out into the sunlight, and into the street filled with beggars, peddlers, tourists, and pilgrims. A dull haze from funeral fires hung over the area.

The Health Officer explained, "Rich and poor alike have their bodies cremated here."

Teresa said, "Then the destitute would come here to die?"

"Yes," Dr. Ahmed said.

Teresa nodded with decision. "This building is

exactly what the Missionary Sisters of Charity need. We will take it.''

"When will you move in?'' Dr. Ahmed asked.

"Tomorrow,'' Teresa said. "It is too late to start today.'' As Teresa and Dr. Ahmed walked away, a monk from the Kali temple watched, his eyes narrowed in suspicion.

As promised, Teresa returned the next day and began taking over the building.

"What shall we call this new place,'' Sister Agnes wondered.

Teresa gave the answer, "Nirmal Hriday—the Place of the Pure Heart.''

As the Missionary Sisters of Charity began carrying sick people into the place, they collected a crowd. A group of monks watched from the next-door temple.

"They appear to be talking about us,'' Sister Agnes said quietly.

The group of pagan monks stood in a tight circle. They whispered furiously and looked up time and again at the nuns. Finally, the monks scattered.

"They've decided to let us be," Sister Gertrude said, relieved.

"Not entirely," Sister Agnes said. "See that one monk. He has posted himself where he can keep us in sight."

After a couple of hours, the monk left—but another one took his place.

"It looks as if they have appointed a team to keep a watch over us," Sister Agnes reported to Teresa.

The sisters grew accustomed to the monks. Day or night, at least one of them observed the activity in the Home for Dying Destitutes.

The second day, Teresa worked inside. As she set up cots for patients, she heard a cry outside. She ran to the street.

A young sister lay sprawled on the pavement. Another was helping her up. The stretcher they had carried lay overturned.

"What happened here?" Teresa asked. "Are you all right?"

The nun stood up and brushed herself off. "Yes," she said.

The other nun explained, "A gang of boys shoved us down. Then they ran away."

"Not the monks?" Teresa asked.

"No," the nun said. She picked up the pillows and blankets they carried on the stretcher. "The monks seemed pleased to see it happen. But they had nothing to do with it."

Teresa glanced at the monk who stood guard. He smiled and looked satisfied with the course of events.

Father Henry came with some helpers from his

congregation. They set ladders against the walls to
replace broken window panes.

"What did this?" Father Henry asked.

"Vandals," Teresa said. "Someone threw a stone
through the window last night. Why would they do
that?"

Father Henry said, "The monks believe your activity is an affront to their religion. They think you
are trying to convert people to Christianity here in
the center of the Hindu religion. So be cautious. The
situation can get out of hand."

Soon the opposition grew more intense. Those who
had used the building as a meeting place saw an
opportunity to regain it if they could force Teresa out.
They stood in the doorways, blocking them. They
pushed and shoved as the nuns tried to enter or leave.

Finally, a pair of sisters carrying a dying man into
the building could not get through.

Teresa came outside. She stood there, cool and
determined. "If you wish," she said, "you can kill
me right here and now. But don't harm this poor
dying man. Let them bring him in."

By then a crowd of onlookers gathered. The trouble-
makers hesitated, then one by one edged away.

Some Hindu leaders took the matter to the local
police chief. They accused Teresa of all sorts of crimes.
"You must put her out," they said. "She is a mockery
to Kali."

"I will," the police chief said. "But first I will see
it for myself."

He walked unannounced into the building to make
his surprise inspection. Most of the sisters appeared
to be too busy to notice him. Finally, he found Teresa.

She was attending to a man with festering sores.
Maggots writhed around in the flesh. She applied a
chemical to clean the wound.

"I have come to inspect this place," the police chief announced. The smell of decaying flesh nearly caused him to throw up. He wanted to look away.

"Yes," Teresa said without looking up. "Wait a moment and I will show you around."

"I can show myself around without help from anybody," the police chief said.

He looked through both rooms.

The Sisters were busy washing filth from the new arrivals. They moved from bed to bed, feeding patients too weak to move, giving medicines and shots of pain killers to those who were in great pain. Throughout it all, the Sisters smiled, touched the patients with gentle hands, and spoke words of love.

The police chief stopped at the bed of a patient who was suffering from malnutrition. The man's body appeared to be nothing but bird-like bones held together by skin as thin as burned paper.

"Are you happy here?" the police chief asked.

The man patted the thin mattress upon which he lay. He spoke in a voice that nearly cracked with tears. "For all my life I've lived like an animal on the streets I've never slept on a mattress. At least I'll sleep on a real bed even if it is only to die."

The police chief came back and stood as Teresa finished cleaning the sores. She lovingly wrapped bandages around the man's wounds.

"I was told you try to convert the dying," the police chief said in a soft voice.

Teresa explained, "Only God can convert. Jesus told us to love one another as He has loved us. All people are welcome here to our love: Hindus, Moslems, Buddhists, Christians. When they die they are buried or cremated, all according to their religion."

The police chief left. He stopped outside and

addressed those who had demanded Teresa be put out.
"I promised I would get that woman out of here. But,
listen to me, I shall not put her out of this place until
you get your mothers and your sisters to do the work
these nuns are doing. In the temple you have a goddess in stone. In this building you will see a living
goddess."

The police chief did his best to protect the place.
But vandals and visitors to the temple continued to
hurl threats and stones at the Sisters.

One morning as Teresa came to the home for the
dying, she saw a crowd gathered on the street outside the temple. What is this, she wondered. More
trouble?

In the midst of the crowd, a young Kali monk lay
on the pavement. Everybody stood back as the poor
man thrashed about and vomited.

Teresa kneeled by the young man. "Help me carry
him inside," she said to those watching.

"What caused his illness?" someone asked.

"It appears he has cholera," Teresa said.

Those watching suddenly remembered other things
they needed to do. No one would touch a man with
cholera. They walked away and left Teresa to attend
to the monk.

She carried him inside by herself. The Sisters helped
him to a bed. They tried to make him comfortable,
knowing that no hospital would accept him.

He resented their help. He cursed them. "Why
bother with a dying man!" he screamed in bitterness.

Teresa gave him the best care. His curses did not
seem to bother her. He blasphemed against God. That
did bother her, he could see. So he cursed God even
more as the nuns helped him.

Little by little, however, he accepted his fate.

After a week he stopped cursing. Instead, he praised

Teresa and her workers. As death approached, he asked for their blessings and prayers.

A delegation of Kali monks came to comfort their companion. For the first time they saw with their own eyes the good that was being done. Teresa disarmed them. Their fears vanished as they saw the care being lavished on their dying comrade.

The head monk said, "I will direct our people to show you every friendship. We will instruct those who worship Kali to do likewise."

The next day a surprise awaited Teresa. Instead of throwing stones at the building, the Kali worshipers stopped long enough to leave gifts of food.

The Kali monk died peacefully after being nursed for two weeks in the Place of the Pure Heart.

CALCUTTA

7

Touching Jesus

The taxi carrying the newspaper reporter and his cameraman rocked to a stop in front of the building. The reporter squinted in the bright sun and read the sign at the entrance:

Corporation of Calcutta
Nirmal Hriday
Home for Dying Destitutes

"This is the place," the reporter said. He sighed and climbed from the taxi. He'd put this place on his story list only because his editor insisted.

That morning the editor had instructed him, "Look into this Mother Teresa and her home for dying destitutes. See what she is all about."

The reporter didn't doubt what he would find— pitiful attempts by poorly trained European missionaries to deal with Calcutta's overwhelming poverty. Who would want to read about nuns carrying bedpans and bandages to people more dead than alive? The reporter shook his head. He might write a good story, but it would go unread. Gloomy stories about morbid subjects seldom found a readership.

He envied his cameraman. A native of Bengal with unflagging energy, his cameraman always succeeded in seeing beauty in the most depressing surroundings. Well, he'd have to work hard to photograph anything good here!

He stepped back and let his cameraman snap a picture of the sign.

"Inside?" the cameraman asked.

"Right," the reporter said. "There are no doors, so it must always be open."

In the cool of the reception area they found a blackboard with the number of patients chalked on it. Today the board listed 63 women and 59 men.

The reporter spoke with the sister on duty, who pointed him in the direction of Mother Teresa. He passed through the reception area and entered the ward for men.

In the dim light he saw three rows of low camp beds placed close together. A nun ladled rice into bowls from a large pot of steaming rice. Missionaries of Charity helped feed the patients. The sounds came softly—the rustle of coarse sari cloth as the nuns walked between the rows of patients, and the whispers of sick men and their labored breathing.

As the reporter feared, the rows of gaunt men could not have presented a more ghastly sight. Despite the best efforts of the Sisters, a smell of death hung in the air that the most powerful antiseptic could not cleanse.

The reporter found Mother Teresa just as she received word that their ambulance was arriving with another load of patients.

She made a mental calculation. "We'll be almost full. It did not take us long to fill the house."

"Surely there are dangers to the free care you give," the reporter said.

Teresa nodded. She'd survived frightening moments when serving the poor. "Yes. Once, when I was to give out food at a local church, the shipment arrived late. When it finally did arrive, a crowd of people rushed forward. They nearly crushed me against the chapel wall."

"How do you avoid that here?" the reporter asked.

"This is sort of a hospital of last resort," Teresa explained. "We take people no hospital wants, or people who have absolutely no one to take care of them. Part of the work of the Sisters is to pick up the dying from the streets of Calcutta. We also accept people the police bring, but only after they've been refused by the nearest hospital."

She cut short her explanation to walk outside and help unload the ambulance.

The reporter smiled in amusement at the "ambulance." To dignify such a vehicle with that title seemed wildly out of place. The ambulance consisted of a dilapidated school bus, painted blue and white, with the seats removed to make room for litters.

But grim reality replaced the smile of amusement when he saw the first man being carried from the bus. The man had no legs. Filth caked his body. The patient smelled of gangrene.

A nun explained what happened. "The man is an untouchable, homeless, without friends or family. He fell ill and tried to end his life by throwing himself in front of a train. He lost both legs."

"Is it possible he is still alive?" the reporter asked.

"He's only asleep," the nun replied.

Teresa said, "As incredible as it may sound, some of our patients do recover, despite the fact that they've

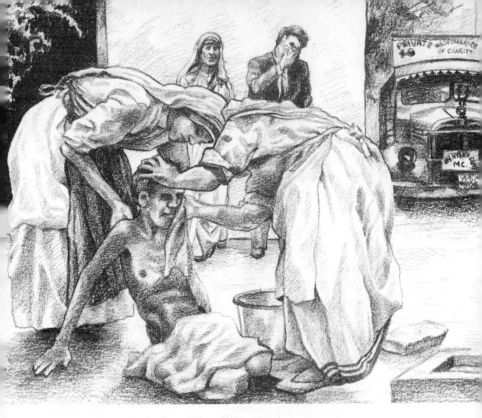

been turned away from the hospital as hopeless cases. Perhaps three or four out of ten do get well.''

The reporter stood back as they carried the man inside. ''I wanted my photographer to take a picture of the ambulance, but he isn't around. Where could he be?''

Teresa smiled, the sparkle in her eyes growing brighter. ''He's probably taking a picture of Sadhana Singh, our new recruit. She's a high caste girl from Mahuadan—and beautiful. Father Harrison recommended her to us.''

The reporter nodded. ''You're right. He'll be with her. Show the way.''

They walked back into the building. As they passed between the rows of low beds, Teresa paused here and there to speak in a light, good-natured voice to this patient or that one. Once in a while a wide-eyed

patient mustered enough strength to smile in gratitude
at the nun who attended to him.

The reporter asked, "How many are on your
staff."

"We have one doctor and a dozen Sisters."

"I expected more European girls," the reporter
said, "yet most of your nuns are from India."

Mother Teresa confirmed what he saw. "Almost
ninety percent of the Sisters are natives. I think that
is amazing, don't you?"

Thoughtfully, the reporter agreed. He knew that
the Hindu caste system made it easy for Indians to
accept poverty as a natural condition. Most people
belong to one of four main classes: brahmans who are
rich and powerful, warriors, traders, and farmers.
Outside the caste system, and so low as to be the most
unfortunate of all, are the "untouchables."

The reporter asked, "But what can you possibly
do for these people?"

Teresa explained, "First of all we make them feel
they are wanted. They learn that they are children
of God. For the few hours they have to live, they have
His love and our love."

As Teresa predicted, they found the cameraman
photographing Sadhana Singh. He kept moving
around her, trying to catch her in the thin shafts of
daylight from the high windows.

"The light is very difficult here. Maybe we could
go outside," the cameraman said hopefully.

Teresa interrupted. "Sadhana must be about her
work. This is her first day here."

"I'm ready," the girl said.

Teresa gave the assignment. "A poor man has just
this moment been brought in by the ambulance. Help
attend to him—wash his face and body. Make him

as comfortable as possible. Sister Agnes will show you
what to do.''

As the girl walked away, the reporter looked at
Teresa in astonishment. He found it unthinkable for
a high caste girl to give herself to the work of cleaning untouchables, especially one in as horrible condition as the man with the missing legs.

"Is it wise to assign a new recruit to such a
disagreeable task?'' the newspaper reporter asked.

"They have to see if this is what God wants for
them,'' Teresa said simply.

The newspaper reporter shook his head. Clearly,
the dear lady had taken leave of her senses. He walked
over to the stretcher where the new girl worked on
the man. Unconsciously, the reporter put a handker-
chief over his nose.

The man, awake now, watched Sadhana Singh and
Sister Agnes in wonder. Dirt covered his body so
thickly it had to be scraped off. Some sores teamed
with maggots. Other sores stunk so badly of gangrene
that even the maggots had died.

"Why are you tending to me without holding your
noses?'' the man asked. "Don't you get the smell?''

"Yes, we get the smell,'' Sister Agnes said, "but
we are thinking about your suffering. Compared to
the agony you are going through, the smell is minor.''

Sadhana Singh nodded, but did not speak. She kept
her lips in a forced smile. She swallowed often. Suddenly she turned and fled.

"She'll not be back,'' the reporter said to Mother
Teresa. "You must lose a lot of girls.''

Teresa said, "Why, no. In two years only one has
left—she found it was not her vocation.'' She touched
the reporter's arm. "Excuse me while I speak with
Sadhana. She needs encouragement.''

Three hours later, the newspaper reporter and his

photographer prepared to leave. As they said goodbye
to Mother Teresa, Sadhana Singh, beaming with happiness, came to Mother Teresa.

"Mother!" Sadhana said, "I cleaned him!"

The reporter, astonished, asked, "What made it
possible? What did Mother Teresa say to you."

Sadhana said, "Mother Teresa told me to do it for
Jesus. I have been touching the body of Christ for the
last three hours!"

The reporter's interest in Teresa's work grew.
Much to his own surprise, he came back time and
again to report on her successes.

"It's a wonder," the reporter said, "your work has
struck a responsive chord in the city. The people of
Calcutta have taken you to their hearts."

"Your newspaper articles have made our work better known. But that has caused a problem," Teresa
confessed.

"A problem?" the reporter asked, puzzled.

"Yes, we have more recruits than we have room.
Our convent at 14 Creek Lane is too crowded."

Father Harrison, the parish priest in Mahuadan,
wrote to Teresa. He asked about Sadhana Singh. He
also offered a solution to Teresa's overcrowding.

"Start a new convent in Mahuadan," he wrote.
"I have a house ready. There's a garden, a well, and
everything your sisters might need."

With Father Harrison's letter in her hand, Teresa
came before Archbishop Perier. She needed his permission to accept Father Harrison's offer.

"The second floor at 14 Creek Lane is full," Teresa
explained to her superior. "We've taken every
available room, and part of the house next door. The
Gomes family has sacrificed far beyond what anyone
else would be willing to endure."

Teresa showed him the letter. "The solution is here.

By starting convents in other cities, trained girls can leave Calcutta. We can take our work to Delhi, Chota Nagpur, Mahuadan, and elsewhere."

Archbishop Perier found himself in an unpleasant position. "Mother, I know you to be a vibrant leader. You want to expand, try new ventures, start new works."

"Yes," Teresa said, "you do see. The need is so very great."

Archbishop Perier shook his head, "Mother, you may not start a new house."

Teresa, seldom at a loss for words, could only stammer. "Why . . . ?"

He said, "It is my unhappy duty to remind you of a rule of Canon Law. The rule forbids new institutes from opening houses outside their city for a period of ten years."

Teresa tried to keep the frustration and disappointment from her voice. "Very well."

"It's a reasonable rule," Archbishop Perier went on. "You need time to build a team of workers, to mold leaders who have your dedication and zeal."

Again, Teresa accepted the decision of those in authority. She tried to understand. "But we are still bursting walls at the Gomes home," Teresa said.

"I'll see what I can do about that," Archbishop Perier promised.

A few weeks later, Archbishop Perier asked Teresa to examine a house and grounds at 54A Lower Circular Road.

Lower Circular Road was one of the city's main roads, in an area where rich city merchants once lived. A prosperous Moslem and his family had occupied the large house. The box-like, three-story building could hardly have been less like a convent.

"It will do," Teresa reported to Father Perier.

"We'll never fill a house that large. But, of course, we could never pay for it either."

Father Perier said, "I have taken care of the payments."

During February of 1953, Teresa moved into the new quarters. With her were the aspirants (who hoped to join the Missionary Sisters of Charity), the postulants (in training to become Sisters), the novices (just newly appointed as unofficial Sisters), and the full-fledged Sisters (who had taken their vows). The entrance was down a narrow dead-end alley, and through the back door. Vines overran the back court and gave some shade from the searing heat of India's noonday sun—all the more important since Teresa banned electric fans from the building.

"How can we feel for the poor who have no fans if we use fans ourselves?" she asked her girls. "No, we will pattern our lives after their poverty. We are poor by choice. We want to be poor like Christ, who, being rich, chose to be born and live and work among the poor."

The list of their possessions was stark. Each sister had a metal bucket for use as a wash basin, one enamel plate, a spoon, a fork, a knife, a bar of soap, a mattress stuffed with straw, and a pair of sheets. Each sister had three habits—one to wear, one to wash, and one to dry. That's all.

A sister could carry all of her possessions with her—her mattress rolled up under one arm and everything else in the metal bucket.

The training of Missionaries of Charity was short—but practical and intense. Sadhana spent six months as an aspirant. As an aspirant she saw the work and learned if it was for her.

After that she spent six months as a postulant. She

learned English and was taught the beginnings of the spiritual life expected of her.

"It is not necessary for a recruit to know English," Teresa said, "but she must have the desire and ability to learn it."

"Why English?" Sadhana asked.

Teresa explained, "One reason is because India has dozens of languages. It would not do to have so many languages being used in one house. But we have another reason for English, a more important one. No other language has as many books for spiritual training and Bible study."

After the first year, Sadhana became a novice for two years. In addition to the work among the poor, she undertook intensive spiritual training in theology, Church history, and Scriptures.

Teresa taught by her words and by her example.

For two years she watched over her novice. Then it came time for Sadhana Singh to take her vows. The entire congregation knelt in the chapel for prayers. The clamor of the city washed through the open windows and drowned out the sound of their voices.

But the sisters weren't praying to be heard by human ears.

CALCUTTA

8

Sowing Joy

Two nuns walked briskly along Park Street, in the heart of Calcutta. They noticed something stirring at the top of an overflowing trash bin. A naked baby girl, no more than a week old, lay in the garbage.

Passers-by ignored the crying baby. Most residents of Calcutta had seen the sight of thrown-away children before. In Calcutta, parents abandoned thousands of babies every week. The parents themselves, homeless and hungry, lived in total poverty.

The nuns picked up the baby and rushed to Shishu Bhavan, the children's home run by Teresa and the Missionaries of Charity.

People expected religious groups to take care of orphans. Each morning as the nuns made their rounds to the hospitals, they returned with at least one baby. The police brought in abandoned infants along with dying destitutes.

Less than a year after moving into their new house at 54A Lower Circular Road, Teresa saw the need for a place for children.

"It is not proper for little children to be put with the dying destitutes," Teresa said.

"We must make room for them somewhere," Sister Agnes agreed. "Two or three babies are brought to us each day. We've never refused to accept an unwanted child. People know that. Each day more and more arrive at our doorstep."

Sister Gertrude added, "And we need a place to store and give out medical supplies."

"We must have yet another building," Teresa concluded.

Almost as soon as she moved into the new convent Teresa began looking for a place to devote to the care and feeding of infants, orphans, and handicapped children. She found an empty house on Creek Lane not far from the Gomes home. She rented it and opened the children's home.

Shishu Bhavan was a plain two-storied building. The nuns put a cross on its rough, unpainted outer wall. Children covered the wall with their scrawled names and other drawings.

Shishu Bhavan became not only a home for children, but a place for the missionaries to carry out their other activities. They started a soup kitchen, a clinic, a dispensary, and a shelter for unmarried expectant mothers to stay until their babies were born.

For the first time, Teresa set aside office space for herself and for the two nuns who helped her. Sister Agnes and Sister Gertrude devoted much of the day to bookkeeping. Teresa didn't want to find herself trapped behind a desk, and she warned the others against it, too.

"We must not let our love for Christ sink from view," she warned. "No matter what else you are doing, spend at least part of each day working among the poorest of the poor."

Teresa depended upon Sister Agnes and Sister Gertrude to help her plan each day's activity.

Sister Gertrude said, "A visitor from England wishes to meet with you. Her name is Lady Jordan."

Teresa drummed a rhythm with her fingers as she thought. She seldom made time in her busy schedule for visitors. "Visitors only want to stand around and watch," she said.

"Rich and powerful people like Lady Jordan could do our cause a great deal of good," Sister Gertrude assured her.

Teresa sighed, resigned. Women of noble birth often worked for good causes—but from a distance. "Very well, I'll see her. But not in the office. Tell her to meet me in the nursery. A problem needs my attention anyway."

"What problem is that?" Sister Agnes asked.

"A boy named Raju lost his mother to a sudden illness. His grief is so great he hasn't eaten or slept for days. This morning, I thought of something that might make him smile again."

At Shishu Bhavan, children ran about everywhere, underfoot on the stairs and throughout the many rooms of the main building. They played in the courtyard, and bounced balls from the high gray wall. They climbed on the iron gate. They waited for a visitor to come through the door.

The children ambushed Teresa as she came in. They tugged at her sari, held her hand, and asked to be lifted and carried, all the time speaking in a half dozen languages, including baby talk.

Cribs in which infants slept and cried filled one room. Patient nuns changed the babies and fed them.

The two nuns who'd found the little girl in the trash bin that morning bathed, fed, and gave her medical attention.

The nuns reported to Mother Teresa, "A passerby saw us take the baby from the trash bin. He said since there are too many people in India already, the abandoned baby would be better off dead."

"It is not for us to decide," Teresa said. "Only God should decide life and death."

People frequently questioned Teresa about her intense loyalty to preserving life regardless of the effort. The people would point out, "But India and other countries are overcrowded. India doesn't have room or food for everybody."

Teresa disagreed. "God gives what is needed. He made the world sufficiently rich to feed and clothe all human beings. He provides for the flowers and birds, for everything in the world that He has created. These little ones are His life. There can never be too many children!"

As Teresa spoke, a nun entered, accompanied by Lady Jordan.

Lady Jordan was a tall woman, with a trim figure. She wore a plain navy-blue dress, simple but well-cut. She had brown hair and penetrating eyes.

Right now she seemed dismayed. She'd waded knee deep through children to reach Teresa. "How many children do you have?" she asked.

"About one hundred," Teresa said.

"It seemed like more," Lady Jordan confessed.

Teresa asked, "Would you walk with me as we talk?"

"Don't let me keep you from your duties," Lady Jordan said.

Teresa pointed to the baskets where the youngest babies slept. Most of them barely clung to life. "The premature infants are placed in packing crates fitted with a large light bulb for warmth."

"They are so tiny," Lady Jordan said.

"If they live," Teresa said, "it is a true miracle. Some weigh less than two pounds."

Lady Jordan said, "One purpose of my visit is to gather information so people in England can make clothing for your children."

"You mean knit or crochet things?" Teresa asked. "When you do, remember the size of these small infants. A hat for them should be the size of a tennis ball."

They left the crib room and walked to the next room, a nursery for three-to-five-year-old children.

"These children are orphans. In addition to that, they have all of the usual childhood diseases—measles, smallpox, diphtheria, and dysentery."

A bright-eyed girl with a runny nose tugged at Lady Jordan's dress. "My name is Bamola," the girl said. "Give me a ride."

Lady Jordan hesitated. Could this girl be about

ready to break out in smallpox or measles or diphtheria? She shuddered. But something in those eyes couldn't be denied. Lady Jordan reached down and picked up the girl. Bamola began playing with Lady Jordan's necklace pendant.

Teresa continued, "Some, like Raju over there, suffer a disease only love can overcome."

The little boy, three years old, stared dumbly at the far wall. He didn't smile or talk. He didn't play with other children.

"He still doesn't eat, either," the nun in charge said. "He misses his mother. He sleeps only in fits. He will soon be sick unless something is done."

Teresa picked up Raju. Lifting him was like lifting a lifeless doll. She put him down in front of a huge stuffed rabbit with long floppy ears. The boy ignored the rabbit and ignored Mother Teresa.

Teresa called the nun to one side. "I have an idea," Teresa said. "What did his mother look like?"

"She was a young woman, an Indian. She wore glasses."

Teresa instructed, "Find a nun who looks something like his mother. Have her sing his favorite lullaby. Tell her to devote herself entirely to the child, at least until his appetite returns."

Lady Jordan succeeded in finding a trinket in her purse that distracted Bamola from the pendant. She let the girl have the trinket and put her on the floor. The girl seemed pleased with her new-found treasure.

"We try to keep them happy here," Teresa said, "but it is not the same as family life. Adoption is one answer. But cute young children grow into older ones. Then they are not as cute and are not as easy to put up for adoption."

"What do you do for children who grow too old for your home?" Lady Jordan asked.

"The older boys go to Boys' Town in Gangarampur. The girls stay here until they are old enough to go out on their own. We find them jobs. For some we even play matchmaker and find them a husband. We provide small dowries for the girls because in India a bride without money to bring to the marriage is not likely to attract a good husband.

"Recently, we experimented with a new approach. Five children from the same family were put in our hands. We picked the one with the most promise and sent him to school. As he grows older he can help support the others in his family."

Lady Jordan interrupted, "The nun has found someone for Raju."

Teresa and Lady Jordan watched as the nun carried the three-year-old boy. The nun sang softly to him. He lay with his head on her shoulder, one hand holding a piece of bread.

"Raju is smiling," Lady Jordan said.

As she spoke, the bread slipped from his fingers, and the little boy fell into a deep and restful sleep.

Teresa observed, "For all kinds of diseases there are medicines and cures. For loneliness, the best cure is love."

Lady Jordan asked, "What is the worst disease? Leprosy?"

"The biggest disease today is not leprosy, but rather the feeling of being unwanted, uncared for, and deserted by everybody. Outcasts are found at every stage of life, from the aged to the newborn infant."

A girl walked into the room to deliver a note to Teresa.

Teresa unfolded the slip of paper and read the note. "It's from the Sister at the desk. Come with me."

A frown of indecision faded from the nun's face as Teresa arrived.

"An unusual case came in a few minutes ago," the nun said. "The police brought in a teen-age boy. They found him at the shipping docks trying to board a ship without tickets or passport."

"He is an orphan?" Teresa asked.

"Not in the usual sense," the nun at the desk said. "He refused to give the police his name."

"Let me talk with him," Teresa decided.

The boy sat on the edge of a chair in the waiting room. When Teresa and Lady Jordan stepped inside, he jumped up. The boy was fifteen or so, slim, wiry, and noticeably nervous. He could hardly stand still in one place.

The boy's appearance surprised Teresa. He was clear eyed, healthy, and dressed in wrinkled but good clothing. Clearly he wasn't the usual street urchin.

"What is your name?" Teresa asked.

"Anwar," the teen-age boy replied.

"And your family name?" Teresa prompted.

"No," Anwar said. "You don't need to know my family."

"Is your father alive?" Teresa asked.

"Yes," the boy replied.

"And your mother?" Teresa asked.

"Yes," the boy replied.

"Do you know where they are?"

"Yes, I know where they are."

"Then why don't you go back to them?" Teresa asked.

Anwar said, "My father doesn't want me. He doesn't care about me."

Teresa explained, "You understand that you can stay here for only a week or two. After that we'll have to send you to Boys' Town."

Anwar took a deep breath. He said firmly, "I'll stay with you."

Teresa came back to the Sister at the desk. "Sign him in," Teresa instructed her. In a whisper she added, "Perhaps in a few days he'll feel differently."

Teresa explained to the visitor from England, "This is the worst disease. People have no time for their children, no time for each other, no time to enjoy each other. Jesus Himself experienced this loneliness. He came among His own and His own received Him not. It hurt Him then and it has kept on hurting Him."

"What can be done?" Lady Jordan asked.

"For Anwar it may be too late. The solution is to spread love everywhere you go, first of all in your own home. Give love to your children, to your parents, to your wife or husband, to your next-door neighbor."

As she spoke a disturbance arose outside. A battered truck, painted blue and white, arrived to pick up supplies for Nirmal Hriday. Older children ran to swing open the iron gate. They engaged in a lot of good-natured kidding as they helped the driver load the truck.

Teresa said, "Would you care to accompany me to the home for dying destitutes?"

Lady Jordan looked at her watch. "I have an appointment elsewhere," she replied quickly. Only with difficulty did she keep relief out of her voice. She welcomed an excuse to escape from being exposed to the wretched destitutes.

"How long will you be in Calcutta?" Teresa asked.

"For another two weeks," Lady Jordan said. "I'm returning to England in January."

"Then you'll be here during Christmas. You must attend our Christmas pageant!"

"Yes, I'd be happy to attend a Christmas play," Lady Jordan said. "Where is it being held?"

"At the leper colony," Teresa said over her shoulder.

"At the leper colony . . . ," Lady Jordan repeated. She watched Teresa disappear down the hall. Please, she thought to herself, someone tell me I misunderstood.

CALCUTTA.

Touch a Leper with Kindness

No disease gives rise to fear and revulsion the way leprosy does. From ancient times victims of the disease became instant outcasts. Everything was cut off from them. Their families put them away. No healthy person would have any contact with them. Even beggars crawled away when lepers came near.

Jesus, however, looked upon the leper in a different way. The Bible says, "Jesus put forth his hand, and touched him, saying . . . be thou clean" (Matthew 8:3).

Once, while Teresa walked the streets of Calcutta, she saw a man hiding in the gloom of a shack thrown together at the end of an alley. He never came out during the day.

"Why are you hiding yourself away?"

"I am ashamed. Besides, when I come out people throw stones at me."

"Why would they do that?" Teresa asked.

"I am a leper," the man said simply.

Teresa investigated. Of the twenty million lepers

in the world, almost fifty thousand lived in Calcutta
or on its outskirts. Teresa had not realized the problem to be that great. Maybe the number of lepers
seemed fewer because they stayed out of sight, suffering in silence, like the man in the alley.

Surely someone in the city helped these people. Yet,
after checking carefully, Teresa found not a single
Calcutta hospital which specialized in treating lepers.

Teresa's missionary spirit saw the need to do
something—but what? The home for the dying and
the children's home required her full attention. How
could she help tens of thousands of lepers?

In 1957 five lepers came to the convent at 54A
Lower Circular Road. "We've been chased away
from our work," one of the men told Teresa. "We
have no shelter or food. Will you help us?"

Teresa explained, "None of our Sisters are trained
in leprosy work."

The leader of the five men said, "We know a doctor who is a specialist. He will show you what can be
done to help us."

Dr. Senn agreed to meet with Teresa. He told her
that not all lepers began as beggars. "Among my
patients are many rich and capable people who held
high positions. But because of the disease, they have
been thrown out of society. They live in slums,
unknown and unloved. No one cares for them. They
beg for food—or dig through garbage cans for scraps."

He agreed to train the Sisters for the leprosy work.
"But once they are trained, what will you do? You
have no money for hospitals or for drugs to treat the
disease."

"God will provide," Teresa said.

Teresa directed all of her Sisters to undertake Dr.
Senn's training class.

He told them, "Leprosy is a disease caused by a

bacteria—a germ. But little else is known about it. At first it attacks the skin. Hard lumps slowly form around the forehead, nose, ears, and lips. At this stage a person can still live a normal life.

"But as it progresses, skin and the softer bones are eaten away. Lepers lose their fingers and toes. They may lose their nose, and their voices change to a croak."

"Can leprosy be cured?" a Sister asked.

"New drugs from the United States and from England can stop the disease and in some cases restore lepers to full health. But they must come to us at once. If they come in time, as soon as they discover a patch of leprosy on their body, they have every opportunity to be completely cured.

"Unfortunately, treatment is long. My patients often grow discouraged and give up before their treatment is finished."

One gray morning at the end of his training class, Dr. Senn arranged a tour to Titagarh, a leper shanty-town on the edge of the city. Titagarh was an industrial area, the site of paper and burlap mills.

Dr. Senn pointed along the railroad right-of-way. "The camp stretches out in both directions along the railroad track. The train company owns the land, but they let the lepers stay, provided the buildings don't become too permanent."

As he spoke, a train rushed by, shaking the flimsy bamboo buildings and causing tin roofs to rattle. Lepers scrambled off the embankment.

Over the roar of the locomotive, Dr. Senn motioned them inside the largest building, a building with thatched roof and packed dirt floor. A hodgepodge of broken chairs, propped-up tables, and sagging beds furnished the building. Not a single piece of furniture matched. In addition, the lepers, who needed a

plentiful supply of fresh water, lived without benefit
of running water or indoor plumbing of any kind.

Horribly disfigured people with advanced cases of
the disease lay in beds. People brought mugs of water
and food to the worst cases and helped wrap running
sores with bandages.

"Those who help are lepers themselves," Dr. Senn
pointed out.

A Sister asked Dr. Senn, "Aren't they embarrassed
to have us walk around and talk about them."

"As if they are some sort of freak show? Yes," the
doctor agreed. "That is one reason lepers don't come
in for help. They feel their life has ended anyway. But
I explain to them that I'm working to cure the disease.
It is one of the few diseases found only in humans.
So the bacteria cannot be tested in animals. If prog-
ress is to be made, we must work with human
subjects."

They stopped in front of a wood stove. A leper with stumplike feet hobbled over to the stove, a crutch under one arm. The leper carried a pot of water to make tea. He held the pot by slipping his wrist through the wire bale, for he had no hands.

Dr. Senn said, "The final stage of the disease attacks the nerves. When the nerves are infected, the sense of feeling is lost. Lepers can't feel pain or heat in their hands or feet."

Dr. Senn picked up a tin cup. "Suppose I filled this with scalding hot water from the tea pot and accidentally gave it to a leper. With his sense of feeling gone, he could suffer bad burns and not even be aware of it."

One of the Sisters asked, "Is it dangerous? I mean, is there a danger of getting the disease by being around lepers?"

Dr. Senn put her fears to rest. "Leprosy is not a highly contagious disease, despite the fear people have of it."

Teresa made plans to help the lepers. "The work will become one of our main activities," she said.

Her determination to do something in a big way for the lepers convinced Dr. Senn to work with her. He left his own practice and joined forces with Mother Teresa and the Missionaries of Charity.

Teresa called a planning session at her office in Shishu Bhavan. "The need is great," Teresa told the group, "so our effort must be great, too."

If anybody could do it, these people could. At her right hand Sister Agnes took notes. Now and then she smiled, flashing straight, white teeth. Although she seldom spoke, and only then in a soft voice, the others could not miss the shy intelligence mirrored by her bright, clear eyes.

Sister Gertrude, the strong, capable leader, sat on

the other side of Mother Teresa. Next to her was Sister Bernard, a nun who'd entered the work with lepers as her special calling.

Present, too, were Dr. Senn and other volunteers. Teresa looked from one to the other. They waited, expectantly. Yes, this group possessed sharp minds, medical training, and an eagerness to please. But they all looked to Teresa to come up with a plan that would work.

Teresa admitted, "We do not have the means to build a hospital where the lepers can come for treatment."

"Even with a hospital, we could care for no more than two or three hundred patients," Sister Gertrude said.

"That does not even scratch the surface of the problem," Sister Bernard said.

Teresa agreed. "We cannot solve the problem in the same way as the home for the dying or the children's home. We need an approach to reach tens of thousands of people."

"And there's another problem," Dr. Senn pointed out. "Many lepers will not come to a hospital. They are ashamed to be seen on public streets."

"What is the solution?" Sister Bernard asked.

"Suppose," Teresa proposed, "we take the hospital to the lepers. We'll go out in the leper camps with mobile dispensaries, taking advice and medicines and Christian love."

"We'll need ambulances to outfit as mobile clinics," Sister Agnes said.

Dr. Senn wrinkled his brows for a moment, thinking. "Yes, your idea will work. We can visit the camps at regular intervals and treat the lepers as outpatients."

Then he added, "But there's a rub. You'll need

money for ambulances and drugs—a great deal of money.''

How could Teresa raise the money?

She took a bold step. *Touch a leper*, she told people. *Touch a leper with your kindness.* All over Calcutta the Missionaries of Charity took up collections with that slogan. The collection drive succeeded. Money poured in from many sources.

They bought five new ambulances, acquired the necessary drugs, and began regular trips into the leper camps.

They established their first center at Titagarh. They took medicines, showed the lepers how to bathe and bandage their sores, and even taught them how to perform minor surgery.

Titagarh became their most successful camp. It constantly expanded along either side of the tracks.

It was to Titagarh that Lady Jordan came for the Christmas pageant.

''Two weeks in Calcutta will change how anyone looks at the world,'' Lady Jordan said. ''The city is full of surprises and shocks to the senses.''

Teresa said, ''Even after thirty years, the city still surprises me.''

''You've been in India that long?'' Lady Jordan asked.

Teresa counted the years. ''Thirty years,'' she said in wonder. ''It hasn't seemed that long.'' She shook her head, clearing thirty years of memories from her mind.

She took up her role as a guide. ''This building is a meeting hall and work area. The lepers built it. We treat them medically, but we also teach them practical skills. They learn to sew their own clothing, make shoes from old tires, weave baskets, make bricks, and do carpentry.

"The lepers are a tremendous people. They could become an entirely self-sufficient community, provided they had good farm land for growing wheat and rice." Teresa grew indignant. "People don't want to live next to lepers. Yet, where do they expect the lepers to live? They're pushed onto unused railway property. What the lepers really need is a city of their own."

"Do you plan upon starting such a leper city?" Lady Jordan asked.

"Yes," Teresa said. "I've already chosen the name: Shanti Nagar—City of Peace. More important than the things they make or grow is the fact they gain a sense of pride in doing it themselves. They learn to support themselves instead of begging."

"Where will the City of Peace be located?" Lady Jordan asked.

"I don't know. Someone will need to donate a large tract of land and we'll need to raise the money to build houses," Teresa said. Then she added, "God will provide."

They entered the long, low building where the Christmas pageant would be performed. Most of the people sat on matting on the floor. Teresa and her guest took their places to one side in the front.

Lady Jordan noticed several children, "Are the children lepers, too?"

"Not all of them," Teresa said. "Some are children of leper couples."

Lady Jordan asked, "Wouldn't it be best to let the children live elsewhere?"

Teresa replied, "These people have been deprived of nearly everything because of their sickness. Is it right to deprive them of their children as well?"

Lady Jordan hastily said, "I was thinking of the children's welfare."

Teresa did not accept that argument either.
"Because of their unfortunate condition, the parents
are all the more loving and tender toward their
children. Should innocent children be deprived of
these loving parents?"

"But surely you do something to prevent the
children from getting the disease," Lady Jordan said.

A dark expression of hurt crossed Teresa's face.
"Some children do contract leprosy from their
parents. That is all the more tragic because medicines
to render the parents noninfectious do exist."

"The medicine must be terribly expensive," Lady
Jordan said,

"No," Teresa said. "Medicines for such treatment
cost less than the small toys the children get as
presents."

"And how are the children at Shishu Bhavan?"
Lady Jordan asked.

"The little girl found in the trash bin is three weeks
old and growing stronger," Teresa answered. "The
Sisters named her Christina and call her their little
niece. They're becoming much too attached to her,
which will cause a problem when she is adopted.

"Adoption appears to be the answer for Raju, the
boy who lost his mother. A couple from the United
States have asked for him. A year from now he'll be
wearing a cowboy outfit and breathing the clean air
of Montana."

"What became of the runaway teen-age boy?"

"Anwar? His father came for him and they were
reconciled, for now at least."

Before the play began, the people asked Teresa to
speak. She stood and said a few words. She ended by
telling the lepers, "You are the gift of God. He loves
you with a special love."

A leper sitting nearby said, "Mother, would you

tell me that again, because I've always heard that no one loves me. It is wonderful to know that God loves me. Say it again.''

Teresa touched him and said, ''Jesus loves you.''

After she returned to her chair, Lady Jordan asked, ''How do you do it? How can you touch a leper and smile?''

Teresa said, ''I know that when I touch the limbs of a leper, I am touching the body of Christ. This conviction of touching Christ under the appearance of a leper gives me a courage which I wouldn't have otherwise.''

As the Christmas play began, Teresa said, ''Lepers play all of the parts. Even the singers in the choir are lepers.''

''They seem so joyful,'' Lady Jordan said.

''The poor are often more fun than the rich, who feel they must always be solemn,'' Teresa said.

At the end of the play, baby Jesus was placed in the manger. Lady Jordan looked more closely at the child. ''The baby . . .?'' she began.

The infant in the manger carried the unmistakable patches of the disease.

''Yes,'' Teresa said. ''Baby Jesus is a leper, too.''

CALCUTTA

10

We Do It for Jesus

The fall of 1959 marked ten years since Rome approved the Missionary Sisters of Charity. Nearly two hundred sisters belonged to the congregation. Among them was a girl from San Diego, California, one from Germany, one from Yugoslavia, an English girl, and Teresa herself belonged to a family from Albania. All the rest were Indians.

In 1959 the ten-year ban on new convent houses expired. Teresa was ready. She'd trained Sisters and nothing would stop her resolve for the Missionary Sisters of Charity to expand and grow. The day the ten-year period ended, she opened houses outside Calcutta, one in Drachi, and another in Ranchi. The house at 54A Lower Circular Road became the mother house—the place to which the other convents reported.

Bishops from all over India asked her to set up houses in their cities. Archbishop Joseph Fernandes invited her to Delhi.

Teresa could not have been more pleased to begin work in Delhi, the capital of India and its fastest growing city. At the seat of Indian government, Teresa would be close to the agencies that provided help for social and charitable work.

Teresa opened a children's home in Delhi.

Jawaharlal Nehru, the Prime Minister of India, attended its dedication. As leader of the largest democratic country in the world, Mr. Nehru enjoyed immense world respect. His attendance at the opening of the children's home clearly signaled his belief in the importance of Teresa's work.

When the Prime Minister arrived, Teresa said, "Let us first go and salute the Master of the house."

She led him into the chapel and knelt in prayer. Mr. Nehru, standing at the back, made a *pranam* by placing his palms together and bowing, a sign of greeting and respect.

After the moment of quiet devotion, Teresa and
Mr. Nehru walked outside for the ceremony. The
children placed garlands around the neck of the Prime
Minister.

Teresa asked, "Sir, shall I tell you about our
work?"

Mr. Nehru answered, "No, Mother, you need not
tell me about your work. I know about it. That is why
I have come."

Mr. Nehru's support took a more direct form. He
instructed the Indian Minister of Transportation to
give Teresa a card which allowed her free travel on
the trains of India.

With the free travel card, Teresa oversaw the opening of homes all over India—in Delhi, Agra, Bombay,
Simla, Ranchi, Trivandrum, and Jhansi.

The successful opening of new houses brought even
more girls into the Missionaries of Charity. Most came
from the same cities where Teresa opened the new
houses.

In Calcutta alone, the Missionaries of Charity
operated Nirmal Hriday (the home for dying
destitutes), fourteen free schools in the poorest slums,
six mother-and-child clinics, a clinic for healthy babies,
Shishu Bhavan (the home for handicapped and abandoned children), Titagarh, and the seven other treatment stations for lepers.

In other cities they began clinics and dispensaries,
schools for the poorest children in the slums, Sunday
schools to teach the Christian faith, and trade schools
so poor people could learn to earn a living.

An informal group of supporters and fund-raisers,
called the Co-Workers of Mother Teresa, aided in all
of this work.

The Co-Workers began about five years earlier
when Mrs. Ann Blaikie read about Teresa in the

Calcutta newspapers. Mrs. Blaikie met with Teresa
and explained her purpose in coming. "I represent
a small group of British ladies in India," she said.
"Is it possible for us to help you in some way?"

Teresa, delighted, asked, "For Christmas can you
raise enough money to buy dresses and shirts and
shoes for the Christian children?"

Mrs. Blaikie said, "Yes, this we can do."

After Christmas, Teresa came to thank Mrs. Blaikie
and her group of British women. As Teresa was about
to leave, she asked, "Would you be able to raise suf-
ficient money for the Moslem children's annual
festival?"

Again Mrs. Blaikie agreed. She began raising
money for the Hindu children's party as well, because
she knew that would be coming next.

Soon Indian women and other non-Europeans
joined the Co-Workers. Support came from Christians as well as non-Christians.

In 1960, several of those who belonged to the
original group of Co-Workers left India and returned
to England. To their surprise, they found efforts being
carried out there for Teresa, also. The network of
helpers extended around the world—England, France,
Germany, Belgium, Poland, Hungary, Holland,
Italy, Spain, Canada, and the United States.

Mrs. Blaikie combined the loose network of supporters into an international association of Co-
Workers. At the time it stayed an unofficial organization. A person didn't join, pay a membership fee, or
get a membership card. Belonging came about when
a person decided to help Mother Teresa in some way.
A Co-Worker could offer prayers, knit or sew clothing,
donate medical supplies, or raise money.

Mrs. Blaikie emphasized the importance of love.

"The amount of love put into what you do is more important than the amount of money raised."

Some Co-Workers could not take an active part because of their age or infirmity. For instance, Miss Jacqueline de Decker, the Belgian woman whom Teresa met in Patna, left India after becoming nearly totally paralyzed. Miss de Decker wrote to others in the same condition as herself. She began a group called the Sick and Suffering Co-Workers of Mother Teresa. A person in Miss de Decker's group adopted a specific Sister and offered prayers for that Sister. The Sister dedicated her work for the suffering one.

Teresa wrote to Jacqueline de Decker, "When the work is hardest, I often think about you and ask God to bless our efforts. I have the feeling God always listens to me right away. Together, you and I are capable of everything in Him who is our strength."

Teresa took great pleasure in seeing the Missionaries of Charity grow. Yet, two areas of unfinished business darkened an otherwise bright success story.

For one thing, she had not yet succeeded in building Shanti Nagar, the city for lepers. The Indian government gave her thirty-six acres of good land about two hundred fifty miles from Calcutta. Teresa laid out the blueprint of a complete leper city with space for five hundred families. However, money for homes stayed out of reach. Weeds grew in the empty field.

The other area of unfinished business concerned Mother Teresa's attempts to start the Missionary Brothers of Charity. For a long time she'd felt the need for men to help care for homeless and runaway boys. When a mission in Kidderpore on the docks of Calcutta opened, the need for brothers to help the men there became even more urgent.

From time to time young men grew interested in the work. Teresa, under the direction of Father

Henry, trained the brothers. But Teresa seldom had more than two or three brothers engaged in service to the poor. The men preferred being in a congregation of their own. In fact, the authorities in Rome would not allow a woman to be the head of a religious congregation of men. After a few weeks or months the brothers left for other pursuits.

Teresa faced a double challenge. She had to encourage at least ten men to join so that a congregation of Missionary Brothers could be formed, and find a suitable priest or brother to direct the new institution.

Concern over these growing pains were put aside in the fall of 1960. Teresa made her first trip outside India since coming to Darjeeling in 1929. The trip was to, of all places, Las Vegas, Nevada.

The Foreign Relief Committee invited her to attend the thirtieth annual convention of the National Council of Catholic Women. The Relief Committee was an organization that sent food to starving people around the world.

Teresa agreed to the trip to Las Vegas. She wanted to answer questions about the work of the Missionaries of Charity and to thank the Foreign Relief Committee for helping her.

The Sisters mobbed Teresa as she prepared to leave. In one hand she carried a canvas bag containing her clothing. In the other hand she carried a notebook.

"Are you going to write down your speech?" the Sisters asked.

Teresa shook her head. Speaking in public was an ordeal she preferred not to think about. "I'll spend the travel time writing letters," she said.

The Sisters hugged her and kissed her and held her close. Everyone had to say goodbye and tell her to be careful and hurry back. They cried and said she

would be missed. For a moment it looked as if she
would never be able to get away.

Nevada in the month of October appeared warm
in the bright sun, but in the clear desert climate each
morning began cool and crisp.

The city of Las Vegas was known for its pleasure-
seeking visitors and gambling, rather than for feeding
hungry people. The hotels offered every luxury—
heated indoor swimming pools, great banquet feasts
at any hour of the day or night, gaudy shows, and
the constant whirl and click of slot machines.

Why had the National Council of Catholic Women
decided to come to this city? For some reason, city
officials had offered the Council free use of the city's
vast convention hall and auditorium. The council
accepted the offer.

For four days, the women lived at hotels and tourist
homes throughout the city. Each morning they rode
to the convention hall's great auditorium for early
morning worship. They filled the rest of the day with
meetings, panel discussions, and workshops.

Booths in the convention hall featured work being
done by the women. Mother Teresa sat at the World
Relief display and answered questions about her many
activities in India. As usual, she wore her rough
leather sandals, the cotton sari with the blue border,
and the cross on her shoulder. Some people believed
her to be a native of India. This rather pleased Teresa.
She wanted to be thought of as a native of her adopted
country.

Not all questions were sweetness and light. For
instance, one Sister who ran a high school for girls
accused Mother Teresa of spoiling the poor. "You
distribute food too freely to them," she said. "The
mothers don't really care about their children."

Teresa bristled at the charge. She seldom lost her

temper or showed anger. But to accuse the poor and suffering in India of being spoiled was almost more than she could bear.

She said, "If I spoil the poor, you and the Sisters spoil the rich in your select schools. And Almighty God is the first to spoil us. Does he not give freely to all of us? Then why should I not imitate my God and give freely to the poor what I have received freely?"

The next day Teresa was scheduled to speak to the entire convention. Eileen Egan, Teresa's hostess at the meeting, drove her out into the desert. It gave Teresa a moment to think and pray before giving her first formal speech before a large crowd.

She walked a few hundred feet from the road and sat down next to a cactus plant. As she thought about what she would say, she gathered a few of the cactus spines and twined them into a crown of thorns.

After a few minutes Eileen called to her, "It's time to go, Mother."

Teresa took the crown of cactus spines back into the city with her.

Teresa's speech told of her work in Calcutta. She described how she and her helpers were able to give poor people the love and respect due every human being. Her speech centered on love.

Teresa said, "We in India love our children. The mothers, as poor as they may be, as sick as they may be—cling to their children.

"A leper woman living far away from one of our leper centers had a little child of two. Bhakti was her name. Bhakti means love. The mother thought she saw on Bhakti's body a white spot, the sign of the disease. And though her feet were partly eaten away, and her hands were without fingers, still this brave woman, this loving woman, carried the child all the way for several miles to the Sisters to make sure that her child did not have leprosy. And when a Sister examined Bhakti and found the child was safe, the mother was so happy she was not afraid to walk back all the way!

"If you think the mothers don't care for their children in India, after an example like this, I don't know what to say!"

Many well-known religious leaders spoke to the Council. But when the meeting ended, everybody agreed that Mother Teresa made the greatest impact.

Eileen Egan didn't want Teresa to judge the United States by the neon lights and larger-than-life activity of Las Vegas. So she arranged for Teresa to visit an average American town—Peoria, Illinois.

The choice of Peoria came about because the Catholic women in Peoria collected funds for Teresa's clinics in Calcutta.

Outside Peoria, in the heart of America's farm land, rich fields of corn stretched for endless miles on both sides of the road. Gleaming metal grain bins nearly burst with the abundant harvest of golden grain. Teresa was filled with wonder at a land so richly blessed.

The local people expected a large crowd to come to see Teresa, so they arranged to meet in a high school auditorium. In her speech, Teresa said, "I have come from India to thank you and every individual family throughout the States for the kindness and the love you have shown. We have broken the wall between the rich and the poor—between the highest social standing, and the poorest of the poor in the slums!

"Most of the girls who work with us come from the best of Indian families. Hindu people do not understand how such girls give up their university degrees, give up their homes, give up their social standings, and come down to help sanctify those people that are created in the image of God.''

After the formal meeting, Teresa visited with the local people in the school library. Somebody produced a cardboard box for collections and placed it on a table. Before the afternoon ended, people dropped in almost five hundred dollars. Teresa had not even asked for an offering.

"May God bless you," she said, "for what you are doing for our poor, our mothers, our children, our sick and dying, our lepers.''

Later, when she was alone with Eileen she confided, "I wanted to hurry back to Calcutta and my work there. But I am glad I came here to meet these good people.''

Teresa next stopped in New York City. She went there not to see the city, but to meet once again with Mother Dengel, the leader of the Medical Mission Sisters. It was Mother Dengel and her Sisters who'd given Teresa the brief, but essential, medical training in Patna.

Unfortunately, when Teresa landed in New York, she learned that Mother Dengel and the Medical Mission Sisters had moved their base of operations to Rome. It appeared Teresa would not be able to meet with her after all.

The next morning Teresa and Eileen Egan went to the chapel for an early Mass. A woman in the gray habit of the Medical Mission Sisters occupied the pew directly in front of them. As Teresa and Eileen turned to leave, the other woman stood, too.

Eileen touched Teresa on the arm. "Why, this is Mother Dengel.''

It was true. By divine Providence, Mother Dengel had just flown in from Rome.

"I'm to take part in a meeting in New York City,"
she said.

So the two missionaries who respected each other
so deeply were able to meet and talk about their work.

Teresa thanked Mother Dengel for her good advice
about feeding her Sisters properly.

"And for the sandals," Teresa said, "the Patna
sandals are an accepted part of our habit. The design
has been passed along to the other members of the
Missionaries of Charity."

From New York she flew to London to obtain supplies of an anti-leprosy medicine.

The trip to the United States and England accomplished an unexpected purpose. It opened Teresa's
eyes to the need for the Missionary Sisters of Charity
to expand beyond the borders of India. Poverty and
loneliness could be found in any city, even in New
York and London.

Teresa had undertaken the trip with some hesitation. She couldn't be sure she would feel comfortable
traveling outside of India. That fear turned out to be
groundless. She enjoyed traveling to other countries,
especially when it gave her the opportunity to tell
others how they could help poor people.

But it was good to be back in Calcutta.

The Sisters asked her all about her trip. "How did
you manage to speak, Mother?"

She smiled. "I closed my eyes! Then I let *Him*
speak."

"Did you ever look at your audience?" they asked.

"No, I looked at no one. I opened my eyes and
looked straight in front of me, above their heads."

She asked them to give away all of the goods she'd
collected on the trip. She kept only the crown of thorns
woven from the cactus needles. What should she do
with it?

Teresa walked into the chapel. A statue of Christ on the cross hung on the wall. She stood on tiptoe and slipped the crown on the head of the statue.

She'd brought back from Las Vegas this crown of thorns as her only souvenir.

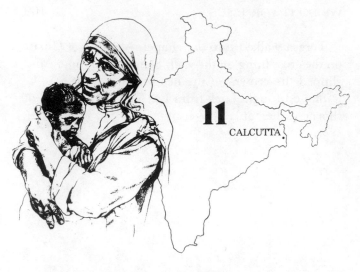

God Will Provide

Each year the Indian government honored one of its citizens by presenting the Padmashree Award. This award, also known as the Magnificent Lotus, was for outstanding service. It was the highest award a civilian could receive.

In 1962 Prime Minister Nehru announced the person selected for the Padmashree Award. The choice came as an unexpected surprise—Mother Teresa of Calcutta. Until then, all people who had received the award had been born in India. Teresa was the first person born outside of India to receive this special recognition.

Unfortunately, some people, including nuns and priests in other orders, became jealous of Teresa's success. They grew envious of the recognition she received. They went to Archbishop Dyer of Calcutta (who had replaced Archbishop Perier) and urged him to forbid Teresa from attending the awards ceremony.

They said, ''Such attention will fill her head with worldly vanity.''

Archbishop Dyer himself wondered about it. The whole thing was highly irregular. He discussed the matter with Father Henry. Archbishop Dyer described his doubts and then asked, "Should she be allowed to travel to Delhi and receive the award in person?"

Father Henry said, "Your Grace, do not fear. There is no danger of Mother Teresa's head swelling with pride. Mother does not know what vanity is. Just tell her that the honor is for all of those who devote themselves to the service of the poor."

Archbishop Dyer asked others about Teresa. They agreed with Father Henry. "She never cared for recognition. She is simple, honest and unobtrusive. Her humility is equal to the challenge."

After deciding in her favor, Archbishop Dyer encountered yet another problem. Teresa herself wanted no part of the award!

Archbishop Dyer called Teresa to his office. He advised her to accept the award. "You must go, Mother," the Archbishop told her. "The award is something that will help your efforts."

Teresa reluctantly agreed to follow the Archbishop's advice. In September she traveled to Delhi for the special honor. The spacious city with its broad streets and imposing red sandstone buildings was less crowded and more wealthy than Calcutta.

Teresa did accept the Padmashree Award—but not for herself. She accepted it in the name of the poor. She said, "You know this is not for me. It is for my people. It is for the poor people who are being recognized. They are becoming wanted . . . loved. The whole world is beginning to know about them."

The award itself consisted of a medallion attached to a multicolored ribbon.

But this success did not overcome the fact that thirty-six acres of good land still lay idle.

How did Mother Teresa raise money for her work? "I go to the people," she said, "to the Hindus and Moslems, and to the Christians, and I tell them, I have come to give you a chance to do something beautiful for God!"

Teresa's simple approach softened even the most hard-hearted businessman. Time and again she received what she wanted simply by telling a businessman how much good he would do donating his goods or services.

If all this failed, Teresa simply waited. She knew and understood the importance of patience. Eventually, God would provide. "The work that we are doing is His work, and He will see that it is completed."

For instance, Sister Francis-Xavier telephoned her from Agra. Agra was the home of India's most famous building, the serene and beautiful Taj Mahal. "I urgently need fifty thousand rupees to start a children's home," the Sister said.

Sister Francis-Xavier had joined the Missionaries of Charity in 1951. She possessed an important qualification—she was a medical doctor. Teresa tried to provide her doctors with all they required. But in this case she had to say no.

"Impossible!" Teresa answered. "Where do you think we would find that much money?"

A few minutes later the telephone rang. The speaker identified himself as the editor of a newspaper. "Mother Teresa," the editor said, "the Philippine government has just awarded you the Magsaysay Prize."

"Another award," Teresa observed without any real enthusiasm.

The editor told her more. "With this award there's a sum of money."

"How much?" Teresa asked.

"Fifty thousand rupees," the editor said.

"In that case," Teresa said, "I suppose God wants a children's home started in Agra."

The Magsaysay Prize was an international honor bestowed by the Conference of Asiatic States. This time no one questioned whether she should attend. Teresa accepted the award in person in Manila. Afterward, she dined with the President of the Philippines and his wife.

In the case of Shanti Nagar, Teresa's patience was finally rewarded, but in a most unusual way. In December of 1964, Pope Paul VI visited Bombay. While in the city he traveled in a white Lincoln convertible limousine given to him by wealthy Americans. The car had been especially designed and manufactured in the United States. No other car existed like it.

After his visit, which drew immense crowds, the Pope made a farewell address at the airport in Bombay. He spoke about the work of Mother Teresa and donated the white limousine to her. "The gift is for her universal mission of love."

Teresa was not there to hear the Pope. As he spoke, she was comforting a dying man in Nirmal Hriday. Only later did she learn about the gift.

What could she do with a white limousine? Certainly she would not use it. Neither she nor any of the Sisters ever rode in the car. One idea did come to mind. She could sell it and use the money to begin construction on Shanti Nagar, the City of Peace for lepers. For that she needed a half million rupees.

She asked a dealer in rare cars, "If I sold the car, how much would it bring?"

The automobile expert said, "An outright sale might raise ninety-thousand rupees."

"Not enough," Teresa concluded. "Perhaps there is some other way."

In the plan that evolved, every person who donated one hundred rupees or more to the Missionaries of Charity received a numbered receipt. After a period of time, the car was simply given to one of those who made a donation.

At their office in Shishu Bhavan, Sister Gertrude and two other Sisters added the contributions. Sister Gertrude punched in the numbers on a large, second-hand adding machine. She pulled the handle and the machine clattered as it typed out the total. She tore off the slip of paper and entered the amount in the ledger. She took the slip of adding machine paper to Mother Teresa.

"The donations have totaled four hundred fifty thousand rupees above what we normally receive," Sister Gertrude told her.

The winner of the car was a woman who had sent in her donation in the name of her son. A few weeks after taking the car, the woman came to talk with Mother Teresa.

The woman said, "My son is away studying in England. I wanted to keep the car for his use when he returned. But he pointed out that a big car like that would use too much gas. It would be much too expensive for him to operate."

The woman smiled happily. "So I sold the car! I've kept half the selling price for my son."

"And the rest?" Teresa asked.

"The rest I'll donate back to the Missionaries of Charity," the woman said.

In all, the car brought in a half million rupees. Teresa could fulfill her cherished dream of a colony for lepers. She gave Sister Francis-Xavier the task of overseeing its construction and running the clinic after the town was finished.

A few days before the town opened, Sister Francis

Xavier asked Teresa to come and give her final approval. Teresa and Father Le Joly took the train to
Shanti Nagar.

Father Le Joly was a well-educated man, the author
of several books. He helped Teresa by advising her
and by training her girls in spiritual matters. He came
to the convent on a regular basis to teach classes.

The four-hour train ride took them through the rich
countryside of India. Fat Indian cattle, totally unlike
the scrawny animals in the city, pulled carts beside
irrigation canals. Women waded in oozing mud to
gather rice seedlings for replanting, while the men
drove water buffaloes and prepared fresh plots of land
for planting.

Sister Francis-Xavier took them on a tour of the
village. First, she showed them the clean, modern
clinic where lepers could be given medical treatment.

"Medical treatment is important, but just as important is the training we will give," Sister Francis-Xavier
said. "It does no good to cure a leper and then send
him back to the streets to beg. We have workshops
and gardens. The lepers will learn a trade and grow
foods."

Finally they came to the houses for the lepers—
little one-room buildings made of concrete walls and
tile roofs.

As Teresa toured the cottages, Father Le Joly
noticed the smile leaving her lips. Something about
the buildings irritated her.

"Why do you disapprove of the buildings?" Father
Le Joly asked.

"The cottages are too good," she said. "Too expensive. The poor villagers who live nearby will become
jealous."

Sister Francis-Xavier would have none of that.
"But the villagers have whole bodies. They have

fingers and hands and feet. They can climb ladders. They can thatch the roofs of their homes and lay on mud plaster. Our people cannot.''

Teresa accepted her explanation.

The three of them walked to the center of the grounds. Francis-Xavier waited for Teresa's final word. Teresa stood in one spot, turning slowly, seeing it all in one wide sweep. The buildings spread out new and modern in the bright Indian sun.

"It is wonderful," Teresa said. "I could not be more happy or more satisfied."

Sister Francis-Xavier beamed, as happy as a schoolgirl being praised by her teacher.

Later, on the train back to Calcutta, Father Le Joly said, "The Sisters have done all right without your daily oversight."

Teresa did not answer at once. She grew thoughtful. She could no longer be everywhere and oversee everything. Yet, the work went on, and usually in exactly the way she would have done it.

Teresa took Father Le Joly's statement as a compliment. With obvious and honest pride she said, "They have been well trained."

When the City of Peace opened, Teresa saw that the moment was right to turn the Calcutta leper city, Titagarh, over to the brothers. Nine brothers worked with the Missionary Sisters of Charity.

Once again she petitioned Rome for permission to start the Missionary Brothers of Charity. Once again the reply came back: a new congregation must have at least ten members. And the new organization should be launched by a man, not a woman.

Teresa took the problem to Archbishop Dyer. "It is a vicious circle. Priests will not recommend that young men come to us unless they can enter a recognized congregation. But recognition by Rome depends upon larger numbers.''

Archbishop Dyer gave his official blessing for Teresa to found the Missionary Brothers of Charity. With his temporary approval they could get underway.

The men carried out all sorts of activities in and around Calcutta. Teresa entrusted them with the men's ward in the home for the dying. They taught boys' schools, constructed buildings, and ran Titagarh, the leper colony along the railroad.

"But the whole thing is temporary and not really satisfactory," Teresa told Father Le Joly.

The brothers needed a leader of their own. He would have to be strong, independent, and forceful in character. At the same time his ideas would have to be enough like Teresa's so that they could work together without clashing. Who could possibly have all of those qualifications?

On the same day that Archbishop Dyer gave his blessing to the Brothers of Charity, a thin Australian man living in Hazaribach was ordained a Jesuit priest. The Australian carried the rather imposing name of Ian Travers-Ball.

Ian Travers-Ball and Mother Teresa had not yet met. But they would.

CALCUTTA

12

A Pencil in God's Hand

In 1964, the tall and thin Father Ian Travers-Ball came to Shishu Bhavan for a few weeks. He shook hands all around. He greeted the Missionaries of Charity with a broad smile that put everyone instantly at ease.

"I am here to see what you are doing," he said.

Father Ian Travers-Ball gathered information for the Institute for Home Studies. He had written several books and booklets presenting the Christian faith to non-Christians. Now he wanted to tell people about the work of the Missionaries of Charity.

What he saw amazed him. Especially Teresa. He wrote, "She works hard. She sleeps little. Not more than two or three hours each night. I think she goes on writing letters until one or two in the morning."

Teresa had been watching him, too. She detected something the others missed. She saw a haunted, feverish look in his eyes. Even as a priest he seemed to feel he was not doing enough for God.

On the day he left, Teresa talked with him about

her work. They walked in the playground. As usual, children ran everywhere, calling to Teresa and tugging at her clothing for attention.

Teresa gently urged him to consider working with poor people.

Father Travers-Ball said, "The poor have not been my main concern. I could never give myself totally to them the way you do."

Teresa said, "There are many comforts that come from working among people who suffer."

Father Travers-Ball said, "But I am too ordinary. I am too inadequate for the task."

"We all have our shortcomings," Teresa said, "but the marvelous thing is that God uses us for His work, even with our weaknesses. God writes through us, and however imperfect pencils we may be, he writes beautifully."

In spite of Teresa's campaign to interest Father Travers-Ball in joining her work, he left Calcutta without any real plans to come back.

However, in less than a year, Father Travers-Ball did return. He still looked painfully thin, and he still disarmed everyone with his friendly smile. To most people he looked the same as before.

Teresa, however, saw a great change. His eyes showed fiery zeal instead of a haunted look. He had made his peace with God.

"I feel the call of God to work with you," he told Teresa. "I want to work among the poorest of the poor in the slums, among the most needy and abandoned."

Teresa gave him her complete support. "Father Travers-Ball is gifted in every possible way— spiritually, mentally, and physically."

In 1965, Father Ian Travers-Ball became the first superior of the Missionary Brothers of Charity.

Teresa's long search for a leader of the men's group finally ended.

What uniform should the brothers wear? Like Teresa, Father Travers-Ball believed the missionaries should move freely through the slums without attracting undue attention. The Sisters all wore the same habit, a blue sari and leather sandals.

Father Travers-Ball decided the brothers would not all dress the same. Instead, each brother would wear his choice of rough-and-ready work clothes—blue jeans or trousers and a short-sleeved shirt.

Father Ian Travers-Ball also changed his own name. All of the other members of his order used the title "Brother." He changed his name to Brother Andrew.

In Calcutta, the number of Sisters continued to grow.

One morning in the spring of 1968, Teresa arose at her usual time of 4:30 in the morning. She prayed in the small, bare second-floor chapel with her Sisters and novices, as she did at the beginning of every day.

Not all of the Sisters could fit into the chapel at the same time. Some stayed below in the courtyard, washing their single change of clothes in tin buckets.

After morning worship, Teresa ate breakfast of an egg, bread, banana, and tea.

In the morning mail she received a personal letter from Pope Paul VI. Teresa opened the thick letter. Inside she found two round-trip airplane tickets from Calcutta to Rome, a check for $10,000, and a letter.

Teresa read the letter. Pope Paul VI invited her to come to Rome to start a new community of Sisters. "Rome has slums that cry out for the healing presence of the Missionary of Charity."

Teresa could hardly wait to tell Father Le Joly. Her face glowed with victory. "Father, the Sisters of

Charity have been invited to go to Rome. The Pope himself asked us to open a house there.''

"To Rome? What a rare honor for such a young congregation!''

Teresa wrote to several Missionaries of Charity already in Europe. She instructed them to make themselves ready for the work in Rome.

Teresa and Sister Frederick left for Italy on August 22, 1968. Sister Frederick was one of the original ten girls from St. Mary's School. She had joined the Missionaries of Charity when Teresa still lived at the Gomes home on Creek Lane.

At the airport in Rome, passengers' luggage rolled along a conveyer belt—leather suitcases, luxurious valises with names embossed in gold, sturdy overnight cases, and a canvas bag with Teresa's name lettered on it.

The customs official demanded identification before Teresa could enter the country. Teresa carried two passports, one from the Vatican and the other from India. With the Vatican passport, the customs official would have waved her on through. Instead, she handed over her Indian passport.

He examined the Indian passport, his lips set in a thin line of disapproval. She didn't dress like other nuns. He distrusted people who looked or acted differently. Finally, he stamped the papers and let them into the country.

After Teresa and Sister Frederick cleared customs, a tall man stepped from the crowd. He waved to attract Teresa's attention.

Teresa looked at the man, puzzled. He looked about sixty years old and stood almost six feet tall with thin hair and strong lines in his face.

Suddenly Teresa cried, "Lazar!''

Lazar Bojaxhiu, her brother, ran to meet her. He

swept her into his arms and began talking in rapid-fire Albanian.

She held up her hands to slow him down. "I have almost forgotten how to speak Albanian."

Lazar began singing a song in Albanian. This song Teresa could remember. Brother and sister sang it together:

> Put your hand in His, in His hand
> And walk all the way along with Him.

They talked and sang and remembered old times.

Years earlier, when Teresa made the choice to become a Loreto Sister, Lazar had bitterly opposed her. He said he would never accept her as a nun. But now he helped Teresa and Sister Frederick into a taxi. As it pulled away, Lazar said, "I live in Italy now. We must see each other more often."

Teresa waved goodbye and settled back into the seat.

The taxi driver asked, "Is this your first time in Rome?"

"Yes," Teresa said.

"I knew it," the driver said. "You're so happy and joyful. You're in luck. I know the city better than anyone else. We are traveling on the most famous street in the entire world, the Via Appia."

The taxi driver, in love with his city, pointed out the ancient sights that made Rome famous: the Pantheon, the Forum, the Colosseum.

He concluded by asking, "You'll want to see them, yes?"

"No," Teresa said. "Take us to the nearest slum."

"A slum?" the driver asked, perplexed. But he drove them where they asked to go.

The taxi turned by a fashionable golf course and turned again to go down an unmarked dirt road. At the end of the road a large number of huts and dilapidated shacks crowded together along a tumbled-down Roman wall.

Teresa stepped out of the taxi and walked around. Children covered with dirt and wearing tattered clothing stared at the two women. The people didn't recognize Teresa as a nun. They supposed she was a poor Indian looking for a home.

None of the buildings had indoor plumbing.

Teresa said, "Send for the other Sisters. This is where we will begin work."

"There's not a suitable building," Sister Frederick said. "We'll need a convent, school, and clinic."

"We'll build them," Teresa said. "There's an act of love to be done here."

The Sisters who were to help in the work came to Rome. Teresa met them at the airport.

She found them upset and worried.

"Here, what is the matter?" Teresa asked.

"We've been robbed," one of the Sisters said. "I was carrying the money—forty thousand lire."

Teresa tossed away her concern about money.

"Don't give it another thought," she said. "It's only money."

Teresa couldn't resist a joke, so she added, "The only thing we have to worry about losing is you. And nobody's going to steal you, you know—you're much too ugly. Now come along and get to work."

The Indian Sisters, as the local people called them, soon made their mark on the community of poor people.

A Rome newspaper sent a man to report on their work. He arrived after a heavy rain turned the dirt road into a quagmire. The taxi driver stopped at the end of the paved road next to the golf course.

"On down," the reporter told his taxi driver.

"This far and no farther," the driver said.

The reporter pulled out a sheaf of bills. "Give it a try."

The taxi driver eyed the money. He looked at the muddy road. Reluctantly he shook his head. "No. I'll not risk my car on such a road."

The reporter disembarked and waded through the mud, holding up his trousers. He wondered if the shine could ever be restored to his shoes.

A stray cat on a roof stopped washing itself to watch the reporter approach. Pigs rooted in the ground, turning up the soil. Chickens pecked around. Clothing hanging on a line to dry flopped heavily in the breeze. Children played hide-and-seek.

The reporter found the Missionaries of Charity. They were hard at work building their convent, school, and clinic.

Two men, skilled builders, did the carpentry and masonary work. About a dozen Sisters helped. The Sisters carried bricks, mixed mortar, moved ladders and scaffolds. All the while they laughed and smiled, trying to follow directions in a language they barely understood. More than half of the Sisters were Indians.

One of the Sisters told the reporter why they were so happy. "This building will be our convent."

"But . . . it looks like little more than a simple shack," the reporter said.

Teresa explained, "When the day is over, the Sisters don't leave the poor in their misery. The Sisters live here with them."

The reporter said, "Some clergy objected to your Sisters coming to Rome."

Surprised, Teresa asked, "Why?"

"They say that Rome already has too many nuns looking for suitable work to do."

"In that case," Teresa said, "my Sisters will show them how to find work."

"What can you do for these people?" the reporter asked.

Teresa said, "The Sisters teach the children their prayers and visit the sick in their homes. They go to the markets for them and get them food."

The reporter asked, "Is there a difference between the poor in India and Rome?"

Teresa answered, "You do not see any television antennas coming out of the rooftops in the slums in Calcutta as you see in some shacks here in Rome. But this difference is more apparent than real. In truth, the poor in Rome, like most poor people in the Western hemisphere, are worse off than those in Calcutta."

"How do you mean?" the reporter asked.

Teresa said, "The poor here in Rome do not seem to believe in anything. That makes them more miserable."

The work continued, but Teresa didn't leave until the Rome convent was established to her satisfaction. Twelve Sisters, seven from India and five from Europe, staffed the center.

When Teresa's stay in Rome ended, friends and Sisters saw her off at the airport terminal.

Each of them brought a surprise bundle or package. "A going-away gift for you to take to the poor in India," they explained.

They pushed upon her a large stack of packages, cardboard boxes, and paper bags.

An Italian customs officer came up to them. "What is this?" he asked. He pointed to the rag-tag bundles on the floor.

Teresa said, "Food, clothing, and collections for the poor."

"You can't carry them with you," the customs official said. "Move along, you're blocking the aisle."

Two more customs men came up. They began waving their arms and telling the Sisters to haul away the bundles and clear the floor.

Teresa and the Sisters knelt on the floor. A crowd of curious passengers gathered.

"What are you doing?" the customs official asked.

"Oh, we're just kneeling down," Teresa said, "to ask God to change your mind so that these gifts can be carried to their destination."

Passengers began laughing. The customs men grew red in the face.

A couple of uniformed guards came on the scene. The customs men argued with each other and with the guards.

After some quick discussion, the customs official

walked to Teresa. He said, "It will be all right. But hurry along and get your packages loaded."

Teresa's brother Lazar had come to the airport to see her off. When they parted he showed his acceptance of her work by saying, "Goodbye, Mother Teresa."

Teresa did not fly directly to India. She stopped in England. While there she agreed to be interviewed on television by Malcolm Muggeridge, who conducted interviews for broadcast by the British Broadcasting Company—the BBC. This would be Teresa's first time to appear on television.

Malcolm Muggeridge had the reputation of being an interviewer who asked tough questions. He'd worked as a newspaper reporter, as editor of the magazine *Punch*, and as a television commentator. Other reporters, out of awe and respect, called him the lion of British journalism.

What happened at the interview is best seen through the eyes of Malcolm Muggeridge. He received word of the hastily arranged interview from the show's producer, Oliver Hunkin.

"Come to the studio," the producer said. "I've arranged a session with Mother Teresa of Calcutta."

Malcolm said, "I know little about her. I need time to study about her and prepare questions."

"I had to set up the program in a great hurry," the producer said. "I've sent a folder of newspaper clippings about Mother Teresa to you. You'll get it in the morning mail."

As soon as the clippings arrived, Malcolm boarded the train to the studio. He scanned the clippings and scrawled a few questions in his notebook.

He didn't know what to expect of Mother Teresa. An interviewer's greatest horror is for a subject to freeze. Nervousness and fear causes some subjects to become speechless as soon as the camera is turned on them.

Mother Teresa waited at the studio in a small room with a table and two chairs. She sat in one chair and Malcolm took the other chair. He held the paper with his list of questions. The camera, lights, and sound men took their positions.

Malcolm's worst fears appeared ready to come true. The poor woman was as nervous as she could be. And she looked so ordinary! She could have been one of the night women who came in to scrub the studio floor.

Malcolm took pity on her. He'd ask her a few simple questions about her childhood. Then he would slowly ease her into a line of discussion that had more substance.

He asked the first question. "When did all this begin for you?"

She said, "It was many years ago when I was at home with my people." She stopped speaking.

Malcolm had hardly looked up from his clipboard before she finished answering the question.

He tried again. "How did you arrive in India?"

She said, "I wanted to be a missionary."

Malcolm grew uneasy. How could he possibly keep the interview going for the required half hour?

He decided to go on to the more difficult topics, so he asked, "Do you not think that the destitution you are trying to cope with in Calcutta requires a government agency disposing of vastly greater resources of money than your Sisters can command?"

Teresa said, "The more government does, the better. What the Sisters have to offer is something else— Christian love." She enjoyed telling about the love of God, so she spoke at greater length on this subject.

As the interview continued, Malcolm noticed that Mother Teresa appeared to be listening intently to his questions. But when he finished, she simply went on talking, looking straight in front of her, without moving her head. She talked about subjects close to her, the loving power of God.

The cameraman frantically tried to save the scene. He kept shifting from her deeply wrinkled face to the cross on her shoulder, to her strong capable hands, to her sandaled feet, and back again to her face.

Malcolm raised another negative point. "In view of the opinion that there are too many people in India, is it really worthwhile trying to salvage a few abandoned children?"

She looked at him with such a blank stare that it appeared she had not understood his question. After a moment she replied, "For man, made in God's image, to turn aside from this universal love, and fashion his own judgments based on his own fears and disparities is a fearful thing, bound to have fearful consequences."

The conversation finally ended.

After Mother Teresa left, Malcolm and the others watched the replay.

At one point, Malcolm spoke. "Watch her reaction to my question about too many children. The notion that there could be too many children was impossible for her to grasp. It was as if I'd asked if the woods could have too many bluebells."

Oliver Hunkin, as producer of the show, had final say about using the interview. He asked the others to state their opinion.

"Not particularly outstanding," Malcolm said.

The cameraman said, "Technically, it is barely useable. The shadows nearly hide her eyes."

Someone else suggested, "Perhaps we can show it late at night—when no one is watching!"

Oliver Hunkin agreed. "The tape is dull and disappointing."

In the end, however, he decided to show it on Sunday evening. The professionals had given their verdict. The program would be broadcast once, and then disappear without a trace.

A surprise awaited the professionals.

Something Beautiful for God

Upon her return to Calcutta, Teresa moved her main office to the mother house at 54A Lower Circular Road.

Sister Frederick worked in the new office. She lived at the mother house and took care of correspondence and details of projects undertaken by Co-Workers.

The number of Co-Workers had grown astonishingly. In the spring of 1969, an estimated 80,000 Co-Workers around the world supported Teresa's work. During March of 1969, the Co-Workers became formally associated with the Missionaries of Charity. Pope Paul VI approved the charter of the International Association of Co-Workers. Mrs. Ann Blaikie served as the first chairperson.

In Calcutta, the enormous task of coordinating activities of the co-workers fell to Sister Frederick along with her other work of managing the office.

Teresa and Sister Frederick furnished the office with a few filing cabinets, two manual typewriters, and a secondhand adding machine.

Sister Frederick suggested installing a telephone. Teresa opposed the idea. She preferred to answer questions by handwritten notes. "Most of my communication with Sisters and volunteers can be carried through the mail."

Sister Frederick said, "Your backlog of unanswered mail runs to several months." Eventually Teresa did agree to a single telephone line.

A few months later, Sister Frederick called for Teresa, "Come to the telephone. Malcolm Muggeridge is on the line from England."

Teresa took the receiver. She had a deep-seated suspicion of reporters. Regardless of how pleasant a conversation with a reporter began, it usually ended with the reporter asking for a special favor.

Malcolm began with a success story. "The response to our television program has been more impressive than I can express."

"What did you expect?" Teresa asked.

Malcolm said, "I assumed the camera would have drained away whatever was real and alive in the conversation. But the reaction was better than I have known for any other program like it. People asked to see it again. We repeated the program quite soon after its first showing. The response to the repeat program was even greater than the first showing!"

He continued, "Letters came from young and old, rich and poor, educated and uneducated. I myself received many letters enclosing checks and money orders. Some were for a few shillings. Others were for hundreds of pounds. I turned the money over to the Co-Workers."

Teresa waited. She expected Malcolm Muggeridge to ask to conduct a follow-up interview.

Malcolm surprised her. He didn't ask for another interview. Instead he proposed to film a documentary on location in India. "We'll come to Calcutta and record the daily life of Mother Teresa."

"How long will it be?" Teresa asked.

"A one-hour show," Malcolm Muggeridge said.

Thoughtfully, Teresa said, "An hour? I suppose I can spare the time."

Malcolm's voice cracked with amusement over the telephone line. "No, the documentary will last for only an hour when shown. But we'll require two or three months to film it."

Teresa turned down the request. "To have a camera crew under foot for two or three months is too much to endure."

Malcolm Muggeridge said goodbye and hung up the receiver. He admired Mother Teresa and respected her. All the same, he intended to change her mind.

Malcolm called together the film crew. "How quickly can a one-hour documentary be filmed in Calcutta?" he asked.

Peter Chafer, the director, said, "To shoot enough film footage, we would need a week at the very least."

Ken Macmillan, the cameraman, believed Peter Chafer to be wildly optimistic. "Shoot an hour-long documentary in one week? Impossible!"

Thoughtfully, Malcolm said, "Filming that quickly will put a strain on everybody. But I think we should give it a try."

Peter Chafer said, "You still have to convince Mother Teresa."

Macolm Muggeridge, however, had learned how to deal with difficult subjects. In the case of Mother Teresa he enlisted the aid of Cardinal Heenan, the Catholic Primate of England.

Cardinal Heenan wrote to Teresa. He advised her

to suffer through the filming because the publicity would help her people.

Teresa agreed, especially when she learned the filming could be done in a week.

In a letter to Malcolm Muggeridge she wrote, "If this TV program is going to help people to love God better, then we will have it, but with one condition— that the Brothers and Sisters be included. They do the work."

She ended the letter with the challenge, "Now let us do something beautiful for God."

In the spring of 1969, Malcolm Muggeridge and the camera crew came to Calcutta. He'd prepared a list of scenes to shoot: home for the dying, leper camp, children's home, slum school, and Sisters in various activities—at mass and in prayer, washing clothes and drying them, and eating their meals.

Malcolm and the camera crew arrived at Calcutta airport on a heavy, humid day. Because of the tight schedule, Teresa invited the crew to stay at the mother house. The crew drove immediately to 54A Lower Circular Road.

Teresa waited for them in the little courtyard of the house.

Ken Macmillan and the sound man set up their equipment in the courtyard. Ken, a first class worrier, found much to worry about. The direct rays of the sun baked the camera and threatened to damage the film. The bright sunlight threw everything into stark contrast, either blinding white or dark shadow.

Before shooting began, Teresa said to Malcolm, "We should go up to the chapel together to pray."

He agreed.

When they walked into the second floor room, he noticed the simplicity of the chapel. Except for the altar at one end and matting on the floor, the room had no other embellishments.

He also noticed the noise. Windows along one wall opened onto the street. The clatter of streetcars and car horns raised a terrible racket.

The noise did not bother Teresa. She appeared not even to hear it. "Prayer is essential," she said. "To keep the lamp burning we have to keep putting oil in it."

She prayed, "Make us worthy, Lord, to serve our fellow man throughout the world who live and die in poverty and hunger. Give them through our hands this day their daily bread, and by our understanding love, give peace and joy."

Malcolm Muggeridge found the praying to be difficult. But the calm assurance Teresa expressed overcame his hesitation. He knelt beside her and recited a prayer he'd learned as a young reporter. He prayed, "Let me offer You in service the service of my thoughts and my tongue, but first give me what I may offer you."

After Teresa stood, he asked, "Are the street sounds always this loud?"

"Yes, but we have learned to ignore it."

Malcolm said, "Our microphones can't be taught to ignore one sound and pick up another. Recording morning worship in here will be next to impossible."

They walked down from the chapel together to the courtyard. Teresa put an ambulance and driver at their disposal. The ambulance waited with motor running to whisk them from one shooting location to the next.

That afternoon the film crew pressed ahead to Nirmal Hriday, the home for dying destitutes.

Malcolm looked over the scene in the men's ward. It was vastly different from England's modern clinics with their brightly lighted rooms and cheery flowers at every bedside. Patients lay on low blue-steel cots. Sisters and Brothers washed, bandaged, and fed them. A Sister clipped the fingernails of a man on a bed by the door.

Malcolm asked, "How many patients have passed through here since it opened?"

Teresa shrugged. She didn't know.

The Sister with the nail clippers supplied the figure. "About twenty-five thousand," she said.

Ken moved his equipment into the room. Some of the patients were unconscious. Others noticed the unusual activity at the doorway. A few propped up on their elbows for a better look at the film crew.

The only light came from the small windows high up on the wall. Ken held his light meter and swept it around the room. The needle barely flickered.

Ken concluded, "Filming in here is quite hopeless."

"Do you have a portable light?" Malcolm asked.

"Only a small one to fill the shadows," Ken said. "But it is much too inadequate to push back the darkness in this cavern."

Peter Chafer said, "Have a go at it anyway."

With the camera rolling, Malcolm asked Teresa what drew her Sisters to the social work at Nirmal Hriday.

"This is not social work," Teresa said. She flashed her unsinkable smile. "Actually, we are touching His body. These people are the body of Christ."

Ken Macmillan was certain the interior shots would not be clear enough to use. He found a few patients sitting outside in the sunlight. He set up the camera out there and shot back-up footage.

They climbed into the rickety ambulance to be taken to the next location for filming. The Sister who

drove the ambulance wove in and out of traffic. The film crew held on for safety's sake as she shot across a busy intersection. Now Malcolm understood why prayer came so naturally to the Missionaries of Charity.

At the children's home the film crew captured a magic moment of love. Teresa held a tiny baby girl in her hands. The baby had been brought in more dead than alive. The Sisters nursed the tiny spark of life back to good health.

"See!" Teresa said in triumph. "There's life in her! I knew it!"

The next morning, Malcolm awoke to begin filming in the chapel. The problem of the noisy chapel still occupied his mind.

He walked into the chapel. He stopped, surprised. The chapel was still and silent.

Sister Agnes and a few other early risers walked single file into the chapel.

Malcolm asked, "Why is there no noise from the streets?"

Sister Agnes said, "The city is on a general strike. Stores are closed and the buses are not running. The street outside is nearly deserted."

"We'll be able to record a sound track here after all," Malcolm Muggeridge thought aloud.

Sister Agnes said, "This is the only morning since we took over the building that the chapel has been quiet."

"What unexpected good fortune!" Malcolm said in wonder.

"All things work together for the good of them that love God," replied Sister Agnes. "Mother calls it Providence—God will provide."

"Do you believe that?" Malcolm responded skeptically.

"Once we ran out of food," said Sister Agnes. "The cook's assistant, a novice, came to Teresa. 'We haven't even a grain of rice left,' the novice said. Mother told the novice to let the Lord take care of it. She sent the novice to the chapel to pray. As the girl prayed, the doorbell rang. An unknown lady arrived at the door with a bag of rice."

Malcolm was moved by the faith and trust demonstrated by Sister Agnes and the other Missionaries of Charity.

He told her, "I lived in Calcutta for eighteen months in the 1930's. I worked on the Statesman newspaper. I found the place barely tolerable. Conditions then were by no means as bad as they are today. To choose to live in the slums of Calcutta, amidst all the dirt and disease, signifies an indomitable spirit."

The filming proceeded smoothly and with unexpected speed. Instead of a full week, they needed only five days. As their shooting schedule drew to a close, Teresa left on the train to visit one of the other houses in India.

At the station she presented Malcolm with a copy of the little manual of devotions she and her Sisters used.

"Our lepers run a print shop," she said. "They printed it."

Malcolm Muggeridge took the little book, then put Teresa on the train. As the train pulled away, he felt as if some of the beauty and joy in the universe went with her. He remarked to Ken, "Something of God's love has rubbed off on Mother Teresa."

Exposed film alone does not make a documentary. Back in England, Malcolm, Ken, and Peter Chafer still had to process the film, edit it together, and mix in the sound track.

When the processed film arrived from the laboratory, Ken anxiously viewed the scene made inside Nirmal Hriday. What Ken saw astonished him. He called the others into the projection room.

"Look at this!" he said. He turned on the projector.

Lovely, soft light bathed the scene inside Nirmal Hriday.

"How do you account for this?" Malcolm asked.

Ken said, "Technically speaking the result is impossible. On an expedition to the Middle East I used some of the same stock in the same kind of poor light. It turned out to be a complete failure."

"What about the insurance footage shot in the courtyard?" Peter asked.

Ken said, "It is dim and hazy."

Malcolm reviewed the events of their days in Calcutta. Was it a coincidence that a general strike closed down the city so a sound track could be recorded in the chapel? Was it good luck that Ken's film in Hirmal Hriday came out well exposed instead of dark and murky? Was it unexpected good fortune that the filming took only five days?

He dared to use a term that modern society shuns: it was a "miracle."

Malcolm Muggeridge spoke after some deep thought, "I am personally persuaded that Ken recorded an actual photographic miracle. Some of Mother Teresa's light got into his film."

The editing of the documentary began. Malcolm needed a title for it. He reread the letters from Teresa. The sentence "Now let us do something beautiful for God" caught his eye. He shortened the sentence to "Something Beautiful for God." The phrase became the title of the documentary and of a book he wrote based upon his experiences in Calcutta with Mother Teresa.

The simple, filmed portrait of Teresa and her Missionaries of Charity often showed the most miserable scenes. But it had a tremendous impact.

Teresa spoke simply, without show. She made no request for money. She did not ask for help for her Sisters. Instead, she appealed to the viewers to understand and love those around them—their own families and neighbors.

Teresa told Malcolm, "I believe the film has brought people closer to God, and your and my hope has been fulfilled."

She encouraged him to devote more of his life to God, "All that you have and all that you are and all that you can be and do—let it all be for Him and Him alone. For Christ, the church, is the same today, yesterday, and tomorrow . . . ."

Something Beautiful for God, both documentary and book, are generally considered decisive events in bringing Teresa to the attention of the world.

Millions of people learned of Teresa's work. Never again would she be considered as only of Calcutta, or even of India. Mother Teresa belonged to the whole world.

Silver Jubilee Success

Heavy rains during India's monsoon season often flooded Calcutta's streets. Sewers overflowed. Shanty-towns in low lying areas became mired knee deep in muck. In the hill country even worse disasters befell the people. Heavy rains caused large chunks of earth to slump down into the valleys, destroying entire towns.

Teresa received word of a disaster in Darjeeling. Bishop Eric Benjamin telephoned the news. "A part of Darjeeling has been destroyed by an avalanche. The landslide wiped out a whole section of the city. Scores of houses have collapsed, some people have died, and many are homeless."

As soon as Teresa heard of the disaster, she went there to help with the rescue effort.

The train carried her only part way to Darjeeling. When they reached the mountains, the engineer brought the train to a halt. He didn't trust the weakened track. The water-logged rail bed might collapse and slide down the mountain as the train tried to pass.

Bishop Benjamin met her in a jeep. "We'll have to travel on the old military road. The main highway is blocked in several places by landslides."

Teresa squeezed into the jeep with Bishop Benjamin and his driver. Overhead she heard the drone of cargo planes as they labored to bring supplies to the damaged city. The one-lane military road wove and twisted through the mountains.

They came around a sharp turn. A truck loomed before them, coming head-on. The jeep driver tried to avoid an accident. He swerved and slammed on the brakes. Too late! Jeep and truck collided.

The crash threw Teresa violently against the windshield.

Bishop Benjamin and his driver recovered first.

"Are you all right?" Bishop Benjamin asked Teresa. He bent over her and observed her closely.

Dazed, she felt above her eye. Blood seeped through the part of the sari that covered her head. "It is only a little cut," Teresa said.

Despite her protests to the contrary, the injury looked serious. Bishop Benjamin became attentive to her condition. He urged the truck and jeep drivers to get their vehicles apart.

They rushed Teresa to the Planter's Hospital in Darjeeling. The doctor treated the wound. Teresa resigned herself to the flurry of activity on her behalf. But she still made light of the injury.

"Nineteen stitches," the doctor told her. "That's how many stitches it took to close the 'little' cut. A bit lower and you would have lost an eye."

"Is she in danger?" asked a woman standing nearby.

"Mother will be bruised and sore for several days," the doctor said. "But if she takes it easy for a time she will fully recover."

Teresa looked toward the woman who spoke. It was Indira Gandhi, prime minister of India!

Indira Gandhi spoke again, "I flew into Darjeeling this morning to inspect the damage. When I heard of your accident I came to the hospital. I want to convey my good wishes for a speedy recovery."

"Thank you," Teresa said. "I am all right."

"The airport is open," Mrs. Gandhi said. "Why did you travel by land?"

"The price of an airline ticket is better used elsewhere," Teresa said. "I once offered to earn my fare on Indian airlines by serving as a stewardess. But they turned me down."

Mrs. Gandhi smiled, uncertain whether to take Teresa's statement seriously. Mrs. Gandhi tried to imagine Mother Teresa walking down the aisle of an airplane, offering coffee or tea to the passengers and adjusting their seat belts and pillows. The thought amused her.

Teresa did recover fully, although it meant several weeks of lightened activity. She spent the time writing letters.

The Sisters took the accident as a blessing in disguise. As the work of the Missionaries had expanded, Teresa kept going only by her tremendous faith and awesome strength. The Sisters watched in concern as she grew tired and overworked. The accident forced Teresa to take a short vacation while she healed.

Something else happened as a result of the accident. A few months after Indira Gandhi spoke with Teresa at the hospital, she gave Teresa a permanent pass for travel on the airlines of India. Mrs. Gandhi told Teresa, "The pass will spare you much time and fatigue."

With the airline pass Teresa could fly anywhere in India at a day's notice. The pass was a mark of respect, too. Usually, only India's most important government officials received such passes.

However, her new position as a public figure did cause difficult moments. She was asked to give her views on almost every important issue confronting India. But Teresa's speciality was love, not politics or social philosophy.

When an issue did concern her, she spoke forcefully. For instance, she attacked the problem of abortion and abandoned children.

"A child is a gift of God," she told anybody who would listen. "If you do not want him, give him to me. I will look after him. But don't murder him!"

Teresa became a mother to more than 10,000 children in twelve homes throughout India.

Caring for orphans took money. Despite their strict

poverty, the ministries of the Missionaries of Charity prospered. Where did the money come from?

"God is my banker," Teresa told Father Le Joly. "Money . . . I never think of it. It always comes. The Lord sends it. We do His work; He provides the means. If He does not give us the means, that shows He does not want the work. So why worry?"

Teresa did experience a few failures, however. One of the most humiliating defeats took place in Northern Ireland.

In that country, politics and religion had become mixed in a most dreadful way. Both Catholic and Protestant groups preached hatred against the other. Terrorists burned buildings, bombed cars, and killed innocent people.

After spending several weeks with the Sisters in London in the autumn of 1971, Teresa made a surprise visit to strife-torn Belfast in Northern Ireland.

Teresa talked to British soldiers trying to keep peace. She prayed with Irish women. She paid a call on Reverend Ian Paisley, the Protestant leader.

Teresa came back to Northern Ireland a year later. She brought with her four Sisters to open a house in Belfast.

"My goal," she announced, "is to unite Protestants and Catholics through deeds of charity."

It didn't work. Neither side budged from their deep-seated fear and hatred of each other. Both Protestants and Catholics criticized the Sisters and looked upon them as outsiders.

If rocks had been thrown, or the Sisters threatened, it would have called attention to the terrible state of Christian love in Northern Ireland. But that didn't happen. Instead, the Sisters suffered the worst of all possible fates.

The people of Belfast simply ignored them.

After two years, Teresa realized the soil in Northern Ireland was not right for planting. She recalled the Sisters and closed the Belfast center.

October 7, 1975, marked the silver Jubilee of the Missionaries of Charity. Exactly twenty-five years earlier Rome approved the congregation. The event called for a special observance.

Teresa wanted a party. "Not for myself," she said to Father Le Joly, "but for the poor. I would like to give every one of my poor a present of some kind."

The Indians loved movies. Teresa planned to show the religious epic *Ben Hur* in one of Calcutta's finest theaters.

"But who will pay for it?" Father Le Joly asked.

"The rich will buy the tickets," she proposed, "but the poor will attend."

On the actual silver Jubilee day, Teresa herself attended a simple ceremony in the mother house. Her glowing face clearly revealed the obvious and honest pleasure she felt.

She had another reason for happiness. Teresa received an award usually reserved only for scientists.

For several years the Food and Agriculture Organization of the United Nations honored the person who increased agricultural production and raised the standard of living throughout the world. The FAO usually gave the award, called the Ceres Medal after the goddess of grain, to a distinguished scientist who developed better farming or food production methods.

But for Teresa they made an exception. The organization presented the medal to Teresa for her commitment to the hungry and poor of the world. The medal carried a sculpture of Teresa on one side. On the other side it showed two hands reaching to set a bowl of food before a starving child.

The Jubilee provided a good time to look back on

the growth of the Missionary Sisters of Charity. The order began with only ten timid and inexperienced girls. By 1975 the Sisters numbered more than 1100. They built the congregation into one of the strongest and fastest growing orders in the Catholic church. The Sisters operated houses in London, Rome, Melbourne, Los Angeles, Harlem, Lima, Yeman, Tanzania, and 73 other places. Their houses circled the world.

On Jubilee day, the Sisters all around the world met and joyfully sang songs of gratitude, prayed to God for His blessing, and expressed their thanksgiving. Then they walked out to care for a million patients at 200 dispensaries, treat 50,000 victims of leprosy at 50 clinics, and comfort 3,400 dying destitutes in 23 houses.

When it all began in Moti Jheel, Teresa had to defend her work. She called her efforts "a drop in the ocean."

"We will never be able to care for all orphans, cure all disease, feed all the hungry, or treat all the lepers," she admitted. "Our purpose is not to cure the world's problems, but to demonstrate Christian love."

However, in 1975, opinion switched completely around. Newspaper reports, magazine articles, and television programs began a drumbeat of praise. They no longer thought of her work as only a drop in the ocean. One magazine called her a "living saint." They could hardly say enough about the great things she accomplished.

Teresa, humble as ever, dismissed the attention. "If you know who you are, then nothing will bother you, neither praise nor slander."

Every day people with good causes flocked to make appointments to talk with her.

"I dislike turning them away," Teresa told her long-time faithful assistant Sister Agnes.

"But if you agree to make appointments with everyone, your entire day will be taken in meeting the public," Sister Agnes said.

Teresa found a solution. She remembered a grand old man of India, Dr. B. C. Roy, a doctor and a politician. Each morning Dr. Roy set aside an hour for free consultation, on a first come, first serve basis. This was an old Indian tradition, called "darshan," where those in power opened their doors to the common people. Anybody could come through Dr. Roy's door during darshan.

Teresa adopted the same custom. She made herself available to any who wished to meet and talk with her. If the person asked her to do something within her power, then she did it.

Some came simply to be in her presence for a few minutes. A crippled boy said, "I am here because Mother loves me."

Two well-dressed businessmen asked for her signature, giving her ten blank sheets of paper to sign. Teresa suspected that the men intended to sell the autographs and make a profit. But it didn't matter. She signed the sheets.

One man brought a garland as a gift. He bowed down and touched her feet in tribute.

"Here," Teresa said, "none of that." She lifted him up. She didn't want people to pay homage to her. If a person looked as if he was about to bow to the ground, Teresa would quickly forestall it by giving him the Indian greeting of folded hands.

In 1979, exciting news reached the Sisters at the mother house in Calcutta.

"Mother has been nominated for the Nobel Peace

Prize," Sister Agnes announced. "The award carries tremendous prestige."

"And $190,000 in cash," Sister Frederick said. Teresa, however, cautioned them against false hope. "I am only one of more than fifty who have been nominated," she said. "The others are wiser, better trained, and more educated."

The Nobel prizes began when Alfred Nobel, the inventor of dynamite, provided in his will for a series of prizes to be awarded each year. One of the prizes would go to the person who had done the most to help the cause of world peace.

Henri Dunant, the founder of the Red Cross, received the first Peace Prize in 1901. President Woodrow Wilson received the award, as did Albert Schweitzer, the medical doctor, and Martin Luther King, Jr., the champion of civil rights. The Nobel Prize for Peace is generally considered the greatest honor the world can bestow upon an individual.

The mother house buzzed with speculation about the award.

"President Jimmy Carter has been nominated, too," someone said.

"When will we know who has won?"

"In October, I think."

"Does Mother have a chance?"

"Of course she does!"

"No," Sister Frederick said emphatically. "It is not certain at all."

"Why not?" a Sister asked.

Sister Frederick explained, "Most winners of the Peace Prize have been involved in politics, economic development, and civil rights."

It was true. People who won the Peace Prize did so because they tried to change the structure of society in some way. That was not for Teresa.

"I am called to help the individual," Teresa said, "not to deal with institutions."

Others believed Teresa to have a good chance. The year before, Egyptian President Anwar Sadat and Israeli Premier Manachem Begin won the prize for their Middle East peace efforts.

Security had become a problem. Those in charge moved the award ceremony from Oslo University to a high-walled medieval fortress. The ceremony took place amid bomb searches, hovering helicopters, and guards carrying machine guns. Such security precautions would not be needed for Teresa.

The five-member Nobel Committee which met throughout the year in Oslo, Norway, would make the final decision. The announcement would be made in October, with the award being made in December.

During October, each time the telephone rang, Sister Frederick jumped. Although Teresa tried to be aloof, she felt the growing tension, too.

Finally the suspense ended. On October 22, the Committee awarded the 1979 Nobel Prize for Peace to Mother Teresa of Calcutta. She was 69 years old.

In explaining the choice, the Nobel Committee said, "Poverty and hunger and distress also constitute a threat to peace."

Calcutta's largest newspaper carried the headline: "The Mother of Bengal is now the Mother of the world."

"Personally, I am unworthy," Teresa responded. "I accept in the name of the poor, because I believe that by giving me the prize the committee is recognizing the presence of the poor in the world."

Well-wishers mobbed the mother house; friends, tourists, officials, photographers, and strangers. They all pressed forward to meet Teresa.

The constant clamor and attention became too

much. "Last night it was as if vultures had descended," Teresa said to Sister Agnes. Then she caught herself and smiled, "But even vultures can be beautiful."

The adulation embarrassed Teresa. She came before the crowd one last time. "I will observe a month of silence," she said. "Silence is the most important quality of a religious life."

In December, Mother Teresa, Sister Frederick, and Sister Agnes boarded the airplane to Oslo to attend the award ceremony.

Sister Agnes wondered what sort of welcome would await Mother Teresa in Protestant Norway. It might be a chilly reception because Teresa asked the organizers to cancel the Nobel banquet.

"Why?" the organizers asked.

"More than $6000 will be saved," Teresa replied promptly. "The money can be put with the Nobel award to build a leper town."

Those in charge agreed to Teresa's request, but without much enthusiasm. The banquet, held at the Hotel Continental, had been a gala affair in other years, with much sparkle and glamor. The people of Oslo always enjoyed the banquet as one of the high points of the week's festivities.

As the airplane flew into Oslo, Teresa nibbled on a piece of bread, a tomato slice, and a bit of lettuce. She jotted down a few notes for her acceptance speech. Her address at the award ceremony would be the most important speech Teresa had ever made.

They landed in Oslo late in the afternoon, the sun already set, and the cold Norway air dipping to 14 degrees Fahrenheit.

Teresa gathered up her cloth bag and stepped from the plane.

An incredible spectacle greeted her. A great line

of people carrying lighted candles welcomed her. The citizens of Oslo braved the mid-winter cold in a spontaneous outburst of affection for Teresa.

In the history of the Nobel prizes, the warmth of this welcome exceeded all others.

A Gathering of Nobility

They came together on December 10, 1979, in the splendor of a Norwegian palace at the University of Oslo. The king of Norway welcomed the guests, who included princes, dukes, heads of state, international dignitaries, and great leaders and great thinkers of the world.

Present, too, were Sister Frederick and Sister Agnes, Lazar Bojaxhiu and his daughter, and some co-workers.

With regal pomp and glittering ceremony the overflow crowd took their seats as the orchestra played.

The master of ceremonies introduced the guest of honor. He said, "Your Majesty, Your Royal Highnesses, Your Excellencies, Ladies and Gentlemen; the Norwegian Nobel Committee has awarded the Peace Prize for 1979 to Mother Teresa."

She stood and walked to the platform. The applause died down as she faced the audience to give her acceptance speech.

She was tiny and slight of build with deep-set eyes.

Her deeply lined face had been parched brown by the relentless sun of India. She wore a simple white wrap-around dress of cheap cotton edged in blue, with a cross on her left shoulder.

She seemed so ordinary! Yet, the diplomats, politicians, and reporters who filled the hall listened respectfully.

Teresa spoke, her voice crisp and direct. In her speech she recalled the events that touched her heart so deeply. She told about the starving family who shared their last bag of rice with their neighbors; the destitute who lived in the streets like an animal, but died under her care as an angel; the small children rescued from the streets by the Missionaries of Charity.

Sister Agnes, sitting in the second row, smiled in amusement because she recognized this speech. She'd heard it many times before.

The speech demonstrated Mother Teresa's shy humor. She did not change her message to cater to this assembly of rich and famous people. Instead, Teresa delivered the same talk that she had given so many times before—to lepers, co-workers, the Sisters, and church groups.

The simple and sincere way in which she spoke breathed new life into the words she said.

She continued, "It is not enough for us to say, 'I love God, but I do not love my neighbor.' The Apostle John says you are a liar if you say you love God and you don't love your neighbor. How can you love God whom you do not see, if you do not love your neighbor whom you see, whom you touch, with whom you live?"

After the ceremony, the king of Norway introduced his guests.

The hand that reached out to beggers in the gutters of Calcutta, now shook the hands of Europe's royalty.

Because she had such deep compassion for the poor, some people thought Teresa would despise the rich. But to Teresa it didn't matter if the hand she took had the smooth, healthy skin of a king or the bony, leather-like skin of the poor. She accepted either one with the same dignity.

The award of the Nobel Prize for Peace marked Teresa's greatest public triumph. She continued to receive awards. But beginning in 1980, she decided no longer to attend award ceremonies in her honor. They took too much time from her service to the poor.

Teresa became one of the most widely known and best-loved women of her time.

What accounted for her success?

At a time when most people believed poverty could only be overcome by spending huge amounts of money and starting vast social programs, Teresa took a different approach. She aimed her energies at specific goals, working with people on a one-to-one basis.

Teresa explained her method this way. "I believe in person-to-person; every person is Christ for me, and since there is only one Jesus, that person is the only person in the world for me at that time."

Perhaps Teresa's unusual ability as a leader explains why the Missionaries of Charity grew at such an unexpected rate. Her forceful personality attracted good workers, and she possessed the skill to develop their special talents. She led by example, and because of her example, people learned the joy of helping the needy.

One volunteer stated, "Mother Teresa can get anyone to help. She makes you want to climb mountains for her."

But what did Teresa believe to be the reason for her success?

"I did nothing, Jesus did it all!"

Agnes Gonxha Bojaxhiu selected the name Teresa,
a choice inspired by St. Theresa of Lisieux
(1873-1897), the French nun known as the "Little
Flower of Jesus."

> How wonderful is a flower,
> It wilts a face that is dour
> And in its place blossoms a smile!
> —*Jonathan Street*

Events in the Life of
Mother Teresa
(Agnes Gonxha Bojaxhiu)

1900 - Nikola Bojaxhiu and his bride, Dronda, move to Skopje in Macedonia (now Yugoslavia). He starts a prosperous construction business and lives in a house near the old stone bridge across the Varder River.

1905 - Aga, sister to Agnes, is born.

1908 - Lazar, brother to Agnes, is born.

1910, Aug. 27 - Agnes Gonxha Bojaxhiu is born.

1913 - The Balkan Wars end. Macedonia is divided between Serbia, Greece, and Bulgaria.

1919 - Nikola Bojaxhiu dies.

1922 - Lazar leaves home.

1925 - Agnes grows interested in mission work, especially in India.

1928, Nov. 29 - Agnes joins the Loreto Sisters. She goes to their convent at Rathfarnham, near Dublin, Ireland.

1929, Jan. 6 - Agnes is sent to India to begin her novitiate in Darjeeling.

1931, May 24 - After two years as a novice, Agnes takes her first vows. She chooses the name Teresa, in memory of Teresa of Lisieux—the Little Flower of Jesus.

1937, May 24 - Agnes, now Teresa, takes her final vows in Loreto School, Darjeeling.

1938-1948 - Teresa teaches geography at St. Mary's High School in Calcutta. For some years she is a principal of the school.

1946, Sept. 10 - "Day of Decision," actually at night, when, on a train to Darjeeling, Teresa hears the call of God. She must serve the poorest of the poor.

1947, Aug. 15 - India becomes free from British rule. Three nations are formed: India, Pakistan, and Ceylon. Refugees flood into Calcutta.

1948, Jan. - Teresa requests permission to live alone outside the convent and to work in the Calcutta slums.

1948, Feb. 2 - Archbishop Perier of Calcutta writes to Rome in behalf of Teresa.

1948, Apr. 12 - Pope Pius XII authorizes Teresa to leave the Sisters of Loreto. She is to remain a nun who reports directly to the Archbishop of Calcutta.

1948, Aug. 8 - Teresa goes to Patna to the American Medical Missionary Sisters for three months of intensive medical training.

1948, Dec. 21 - Teresa returns to Calcutta. She opens her first slum work in Moti Jheel.

1948 - Teresa becomes an Indian citizen.

1949, Feb. - Teresa moves into the second floor flat at 14 Creek Lane, the home of the Gomes family.

1949, Mar. 19 - Subhasini Das, a young Bengali girl, becomes the first to join Mother Teresa. Subhasini Das will eventually take the name Sister Agnes.

1950, Oct. 7 - The new congregation of the Missionary Sisters of Charity is approved.

1952, Feb. - The Missionary Sisters of Charity outgrow their headquarters in the Gomes home. They move to 54A Lower Circular Road, a three-story building.

1952, Aug.22 - Nirmal Hriday (The Place of Pure Heart) for dying destitutes is opened next door to the temple of the goddess Kali.

1953, Apr. - The first group of Missionary Sisters of Charity take their first vows.

1955 - Shishu Bhavan, the children's home for abandoned and handicapped children, is opened.

1957 - Teresa starts working with the lepers of Calcutta.

1959 - The first houses outside of Calcutta are opened.

1960, Oct. - Teresa travels outside of India for the first time since coming there in 1929. She addresses the National Council of Catholic Women in Las Vegas, Nevada.

1962, Sept. - Teresa receives the Padmashree Award (Magnificent Lotus) from the government of India.

1963, Mar. 25 - The Archbishop of Calcutta blesses the beginning of a new branch, the Missionary Brothers of Charity.

1965 - Shanti Nagar, the City of Peace for Lepers, is opened.

1965 - Father Ian Travers-Ball becomes leader of the Missionary Brothers of Charity. He takes the name Brother Andrew.

1968, Aug. 22 - Teresa goes to Rome to open a center in the slums of that city.

1969, Mar. 26 - The International Association of Co-Workers of Mother Teresa is affiliated on a formal basis with the Missionaries of Charity.

1970, Dec. 8 - A convent is opened in London to train novices from Europe and the Americas.

1971, Jan. 6 - Pope Paul VI awards Teresa the Pope John XIII Peace Prize.

1971, Oct. - A house is opened in Belfast, Northern Ireland.

1971, Oct. 19 - A house is opened in Bronx, New York.

1973, Aug. - The convent in London for training novices is transferred to Rome.

1973, Sept. 18 - The house in Belfast is closed.

1975, Aug. - The United Nations Food and Agricultural Organization awards Teresa the Ceres Medal in recognition of her commitment to the hungry and poor of the world.

1979, Dec. - Mother Teresa is awarded the Nobel Prize for Peace.

1980 - The Missionary Sisters and Brothers of Charity has 1800 sisters, 250 brothers, and 150,000 co-workers. They have houses in 70 countries.

1980, Mar. 22 - Mother Teresa is awarded the Bharat Ratna (Jewel of India) by the government of India. She decides no longer to attend ceremonies for awards in her honor because the ceremonies take too much time from her service to the poorest of the poor.

BIBLIOGRAPHY

J. Cummings, "Stubborn Fighter For The Poorest Of The Poor," NY Times Biography Service (Oct. 1979) 10:1439-40.

Desmond Doig, *Mother Teresa, Her People and Her Work* (San Francisco: Harper & Row, 1976).

Eileen Egan, *The Works of Peace* (NY: Sheed and Ward, 1965).

_____, "Mother Teresa, The Myth and the Person," *America* (22 Mar. 1980) 142:1239-43.

John. E. Frazer, "Mother to the Poorest of the Poor," *Reader's Digest* (Mar. 1973) 102:141-4.

George Gorree and Jean Barbier, *Love Without Boundaries: Mother Teresa of Calcutta* (Huntington, IN: Our Sunday Visitor, Inc., 1974).

Jose Gonzales-Balado, *Always the Poor — Mother Teresa: Her Life and Message* (Liguori, MO: Liguori Publication, 1980).

M. T. Kaufman, "World of Mother Teresa," *NY Times Magazine,* (9 Dec. 1979) pp. 42-5 + .

Edward Le Joly, *Servant of Love: Mother Teresa and Her Missionaries of Charity* (San Francisco: Harper & Row, 1977).

James McGovern, *To Give the Love of Christ; A Portrait of Mother Teresa and the Missionaries of Charity* (NY: Paulist Press, 1978).

Malcolm Muggeridge, *Something Beautiful for God* (San Francisco: Harper & Row, 1971).

"Nobel Prizes," *Time* (Oct. 29, 1979) 114:87.

Daphine Rae, *Love Until It Hurts* (San Francisco: Harper & Row, 1981).

"Saints Among Us," *Time* (Dec. 29, 1975) 106:47-9 + .

Robert Serrou, *Teresa of Calcutta: A Pictorial Biography* (NY: McGraw-Hill Book Co., 1980).

Mother Teresa, *A Gift for God, Prayers and Meditations* (San Francisco: Harper & Row, 1975).

Mother Teresa: Missionary of Love. (Canfield, OH: Alba House Communications, 1981). This is a filmstrip and audio cassette package.

Mother Teresa speaking at the 41st Eucharistic Congress, "Response of the Church to the Poor" (Ann Arbor, MI: Congress Cassettes, 1976) Audio cassette #302.

Mother Teresa speaking at the 41st Eucharistic Congress, "Woman and the Eucharist" (Ann Arbor, MI: Congress Cassettes, 1976) Audio cassette #702.

Mother Teresa speaking at the National Presbyterian Church, Washington, D.C. (Rochester, MN: Co-Workers of Mother Teresa in America, Inc., 1974) Audio cassette.

Mother Teresa speaking at the National Shrine of the Immaculate Conception in Washington, D.C., and the College of Notre Dame, Baltimore, MD (Rochester, MN: Co-Workers of Mother Teresa in America, Inc., 1975) Audio Cassette.

K. L. Woodward and others, "Nobel Laureates," *Newsweek* (Oct. 29, 1979) 24:60.

The World of Mother Teresa (NY: Ann Petrie Productions, 1981) 16mm color film.

INDEX

SOWER SERIES

ATHLETE
Billy Sunday, Home Run to Heaven
by Robert Allen

BUSINESSMAN
Clinton B. Fisk, Defender of the Downtrodden
by W. F. Pindell

EXPLORERS AND PIONEERS
Christopher Columbus, Adventurer of Faith and Courage
by Bennie Rhodes

HOMEMAKERS
Abigail Adams, First Lady of Faith and Courage
by Evelyn Witter
Susanna Wesley, Mother of John and Charles
by Charles Ludwig

HUMANITARIANS
Jane Addams, Founder of Hull House
by David Collins
Florence Nightingale, God's Servant at the Battlefield
by David Collins
Teresa of Calcutta, Serving the Poorest of the Poor
by D. Jeanene Watson
Clara Barton, God's Soldier of Mercy
by David Collins

MUSICIANS AND POETS

Mahalia Jackson, Singer for God
by Evelyn Witter

Francis Scott Key, God's Courageous Composer
by David Collins

SCIENTISTS

George Washington Carver, Man's Slave Becomes God's
Scientist, by David Collins

Samuel F.B. Morse, Artist with a Message
by John Hudson Tiner

Johannes Kepler, Giant of Faith and Science
by John Hudson Tiner

Isaac Newton, Inventor, Scientist, and Teacher
by John Hudson Tiner

The Wright Brothers, They Gave Us Wings
by Charles Ludwig

STATESMEN

Robert E. Lee, Gallant Christian Soldier
by Lee Roddy

Abraham Lincoln, God's Leader for a Nation
by David Collins

George Washington, Man of Prayer and Courage
by Norma Cournow Camp